CHAPTER ONE

After breakfast one morning when I was 4, to relieve an intense stomach pain, I first had to double over while cradling my gut and when that didn't help I tried rolling back and forth over the floor. Dad rushed me to a doctor. In 1930 a burst appendix was certain death because antibiotics didn't exist. If it had burst, you wouldn't be reading this book.

Such an event illustrates how the course of one's life can turn abruptly. One day when I was 4, I seemed healthy, and the next morning, near death. Sudden life changes have been a pattern for me — consign it to fate, coincidence or the divine, but I am who I am because of them. Fortunately, for most of my life, I have been able to latch on to the opportunities many of these sudden changes created, and then direct them towards ends that have benefited my family and others.

If not for the doctor removing my appendix I would have died; if not for being ordered to pluck gravel out of a side of beef at the end of a work shift, I probably would not have bought my first cafe, the Hidden Inn; if not for a drunken conventioneer trying to steal the porcelain tank top to our basement toilet we might not have taken the next step towards building the first Happy Chef restaurant; if not for volunteering for an assignment in the army I wouldn't have laid the ground work for Happy Chef; if not for a "Help Wanted" ad I likely wouldn't have met the teenager who would become my wife; and if not for being employed by two mediocre restaurant managers I would not have learned a better system. I could mention dozens of other "ifs" but rather than do that now perhaps I should first let you see all the items on the menu of my life.

My grandparents, Nick and Mary Frederick, had eight sons and four daughters, and of the twelve children nearly all settled in southern Minnesota after leaving home. My father, William Frederick, farmed land adjacent to the original homestead and along with my mother, Wanda, raised his own "help" by having nine children. I was the oldest, born April 17, 1926, at St. Joseph's Hospital in Mankato, Minnesota. My parents' first six children, all boys,

My brothers and sisters (Back row: Sal, Bob, Jerry, Nick, Ed, Tom ~ Front row: Bill, Helen, Pat)

were born so close over a ten-year span that their births seemed to overlap: Marcel (myself), Gerald, Robert, Edward, Nicholas and Thomas. Patricia and William were born shortly before I left home, and Helen, three years after.

My parents made me feel responsible for the welfare of my brothers because I was the oldest. Starting at age 6, on Saturday nights, I had to baby-sit my three younger brothers while my parents played cards at a neighbor's farm. What they did in leaving me in charge would be considered a criminal act today. In their defense, before they had left for the evening, they did show me how to bank the coal stove, tuck the younger ones in and double-check everything prior to nodding off to sleep myself. What a fertile training ground for a future restaurant manager.

On my mother Wanda's side was her sister, Frances, and brothers Freddy and Marcel. (Marcel died young, and I was named after him.) My Grandfather Polaczyk felt he couldn't raise Wanda, Frances and Freddy all by himself after his wife died following their immigration from Poland. Not fluent in English and uncertain where to turn, he ultimately handed them over to a state-sponsored orphanage in Owatonna, Minnesota. A Duluth family picked Frances, and the McNamaras, a Madison Lake couple, chose Freddy and Wanda, my mother. The McNamaras adopted Freddy, switched his surname to theirs and put him to work, but for whatever reason they never legally adopted my mother. Her last name stayed Polaczyk.

THE OFFICIAL AUTOBIOGRAPHY OF
Sal Frederick

THE OFFICIAL AUTOBIOGRAPHY OF
Sal Frederick

With Daniel J. Vance

©2000 by AdVance Creative. All rights reserved.

AdVance Creative
P.O. Box 154
Vernon Center, MN 56090

First Printing

Photos for chapters one through eleven provided by Sal Frederick
Cover photo by Kris Kathmann
Book designed by Kris Kathmann

ISBN 0-9672014-1-1

To the millions of Hidden Inn, Corner Cafe, Brett's Grill, Newman Center, Fredericks' Cafe and Happy Chef customers who made our dreams come true.

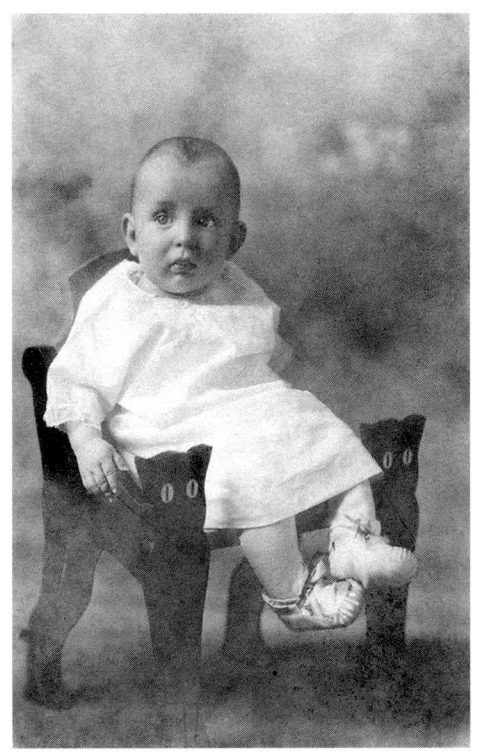

Marcel Frederick, 1927

Sal with the McNamaras

Grandpa Mike McNamara retired from farming the day my mom and dad married. As a wedding gift he gave them a log cabin on his property. In return Dad joined Uncle Freddy in farming the land. (When Dad purchased the farm years later, Freddy moved north to live near his McNamara relatives. It was then that Grandma Ida McNamara made me promise that I would always take care of their gravesite. I was her favorite grandchild, and in German tradition, the oldest, the one entrusted with the responsibility. I still tend it for her and Grandpa.)

During the '30s, our toys were mostly homemade. We had to invent our games. For example, our farm buildings formed a partial ring around the farmyard wherein we could leap from roof to roof for fun or walk the wood fence between them. We had hog and chicken barns, another for Black Angus and Holsteins, and several machine sheds. And a big bull. A farmer learns about fear when a bull breaks loose. One time ours broke out, tipped over a wagon and began snorting at a haystack. Mom and Dad, pitchforks in hand, marched after the animal as the angry German villagers did after Frankenstein's monster. Our German shepherd bravely sunk his teeth into the bull's back leg and the bull ran back into its pen. When you've been eye-to-eye with a bull and with only a pitchfork in hand, such "monsters" as a rival restaurant chain or a political opponent appear less daunting.

We didn't think of ourselves as poor then because all our neighbors had about the same standard of living, but by today's standards we were of meager means indeed, almost third world-like: patched clothes and socks, hand-me-downs, and no electricity, running water or indoor toilet.

Every morning at 4:30 a.m., Mom and Dad woke Jerry and I, as mere toddlers, for the walk to the barn where we leaned against barn studs and drifted back to sleep while they milked the twenty or so Holsteins. Our everyday chores would be viewed as child abuse today. At a very young age I was expected to carry pails of water and feed for the hogs and chickens. One early March evening before Mom and Dad went off to play cards at the neighbor's house, I was told to shut the hog barn door before going to bed to keep the farrowing sows and their piglets from getting chilled. For whatever reason I forgot to do it and at about 1:30 a.m. I was rolled out of bed. Dad was very upset and told me to go shut the hog barn door. I made the mistake of asking why he hadn't shut it when he was down there. His foot on my butt left an indelible impression about responsibility that hasn't been forgotten yet.

Dad was a doer, not a talker, and as a family we imitated his lead, rarely speaking of feelings and ideas. He also had great common sense. Even though he was a taskmaster, he still laughed and people enjoyed being around him. As most Minnesotans did in those days, he pitched in, for example, when a neighbor's barn burned down or an ill friend needed harvest help. Repeatedly, he sent his sons on these missions of mercy, not expecting compensation for the loss of his labor pool, just the reward of having done what was right. (After retiring from farming, Dad began a second career as a Pioneer seed corn salesman. He succeeded because he knew when not to make the sales call, and realized that driving an older car would help sales because his customers wouldn't think he had too much money. I learned a lot in my dealings with him, especially in how to get along with his my-way-or-the-highway type of personality.)

Dad and Mom took their Catholic faith very seriously. On Christmas Eve we always attended high mass at midnight and stayed after it for the two low masses. As my brothers and I grew older and began bringing girlfriends to this annual ritual, we would sit behind the rest of the family because our pew was too small to hold everyone. When high mass ended and before the first low mass, my older brothers and I would leave church and go home to cook the big morning breakfast we always had following Christmas mass. Dad was really disgusted with us at first, but when he saw how much fun we were having and when Mom said, "Oh, calm down, Willie," he joined in to make it a real family affair.

During the blizzard of 1936, in the morning, we couldn't get out any of the doors so Dad shoved me out a window so I could clear the snow from the front door with a coal shovel. Except for Dad using the horses and sleigh for a couple of trips into town, we didn't leave the farm for two weeks during the windy and snowy barrage. We had a hard time tending to all our farm animals but by working together we survived.

Sometimes Mom persuaded Dad to soften his punishment for a particular breech of discipline, but at other times we felt his leather harness strap after stepping over the line. Because I was oldest, and the one who should have known better, I ended up black and blue more than all the other kids. Such punishment may seem severe but it certainly built in us a character trait, self-discipline, which many children today sorely lack. Mom raised most of her children in an enlarged and re-sided log cabin. They added three rooms upstairs and a lean-to on the south side. A couple of the younger kids always slept in a bed in Mom and Dad's room. The Frederick family was knit tightly together during the '30s and early '40s. Is there any other explanation for how four brothers could work as a team for over twenty years building Happy Chef Systems and yet to this day respect each other?

I learned so much from him. Dad would order me off to a chore with only a

With Mom and Dad, age 9

11

minimum of information about how he wanted it accomplished. He told me to cultivate. So I began cultivating like he asked and kept at it until I saw him coming. "Why are you doing it that way?" he said, as I stopped the horses. "You did it that way last time, now go the opposite direction!" Without realizing it, the four Frederick brothers running Happy Chef later offered the same type of direction to its employees. Dad gave us the freedom to fail, which was a better teaching method than leading us around by the hand.

I was a typical farm boy that had his share of freak "accidents." While running through the pasture I cut a deep gash in my knee on barbed wire; the scar lengthened with age. I once emptied powder from fifteen firecrackers into a pile and lit it. The flash burned my hands, and I couldn't milk cows for two weeks, which angered Dad. Another time I placed a firecracker in a cotter key can and lit it. To shield myself from the bang I ran into the granary and pulled the two sliding doors together, leaving a slit large enough to peek through. The can's lid exploded through the slit and struck me below the nose, slicing my lip and face. That scar is still there. While milking cows at Grandpa Nick's a big horse fly bit the cow I was milking. She kicked at it and in doing so knocked me off the stool and underneath the next cow – and that startled her, and she kicked me in the head. I was a bloody mess running to the house. All these scars I'll carry to my grave.

The Frederick boys as Mass servers with Father McMahon

School through eighth grade was three miles away at All Saints Catholic in Madison Lake and high school was a ten-mile bus ride to Mankato. Since the high school bus driver refused to navigate the dirt road in front of our house, I had to move in with Grandpa Nick, who lived on a tar road. There, beginning at 14 and continuing through high school, I had to milk cows, feed chickens and hogs, and gather eggs every morning before hopping on the school bus. Uncle Cletus, Grandpa Nick's youngest, besides running the farm also managed a popular dance band that performed nearly every night at one venue or another in southern Minnesota. His snappy band was entertainment in an era that didn't have cable TV, MTV or even television. The radio signals then from Minneapolis were often no better than crackle and fuzz. With me there to do his chores for him, Cletus could leave for his band engagements just a little earlier and sleep later in the morning.

In my senior year at Mankato High School I joined the track team and ran the quarter mile. Once in a while afternoon practice ran long or we had a track meet and I'd miss the bus for Madison Lake. I'd call Aunt Loretta and Uncle Paul Frederick, who lived in North Mankato, and they would let me stay at their house for the night.

During my life I've answered to five names: Marcel, Celly, Sally, Freddie and Sal. My birth name was Marcel. My Dad, relatives and neighbors shortened Marcel to "Celly." When I started first grade my classmates turned Celly into "Sally," a nickname that stuck through high school. In the army, as you will read in the next chapter, I became "Freddie."

In retrospect, in the '30s we were a poor family but happy. The Great Depression then transitioned into the 1940s and out of nowhere my German ancestors goose-stepped across Europe to begin World War II. It changed my life and me forever.

High school graduation, 1944

13

34th Infantry, 24th Division

CHAPTER TWO

In June 1944, like every 18-year-old American male, I was itching to fight for my country. But while registering for military duty, a doctor diagnosed me with scarlet fever — and not only that, he said I was one of the nine percent of Americans that have it twice. Two weeks later, after the scarlet fever eased, I passed his physical and was ordered to Fort Snelling, near Minneapolis. By then all my friends from the Mankato area had already been transported to various military bases across the country for basic training.

A Fort Snelling officer gleaned from my high school record that I had an aptitude for mechanics and based on that information he assigned me to the army air force. But before he could send me to basic training in Colorado he said I first had to wait in a barracks until enough men could be accumulated for the trip. Since I was the first man recruited for the next shipment, he appointed me his barracks leader, a designation that apparently meant nothing to the other recruits who began trickling in. After I challenged them to stop horsing around, several of them picked me up — all my 120 pounds — and in unison they heaved me out the barracks door. I brushed myself off, sheepishly marched to the command post and asked for the officer on duty. While I was trying to explain what had happened the officer motioned for me to say no more. He led me back to the barracks where he vigorously dressed down the offenders. This was my first experience with military discipline, and it was a learning experience for the recruits.

I had never been outside Minnesota before, and in state only as far as the state fair as part of the FFA crop judging team. Basic training in Colorado was a new and exciting experience. The excitement continued on after basic training when the powers that be ordered me along with 400 others to Keesler Field, Mississippi, some ninety miles northeast of New Orleans. At Keesler Field we began studying airplane mechanics and flight engineering.

While one pilot at Keesler Field was accelerating his B-24 down the runway at about fifty feet above ground, his flight engineer trainee incorrectly feathered the propellers

Basic training in Colorado; I'm at the upper left

which caused the plane to snap in half when the tail flopped to the ground, resulting in only a few bumps and bruises to the flight crew, but leaving a few bruised egos. The trainee's mistake caught everyone's attention. The B-24 was the workhorse of most WWII bombing runs yet never received due credit, especially when compared to its famous cousin, the B-17. One-third more B-24s flew than B-17s. They were twin-tailed, shorter and wider, and like the B-17 had belly and top gunners along with nose and tail gunners.

Fifteen days before what was to be graduation day the air force suddenly shut down our flight engineering school at Keesler Field and ordered us all to Camp Howze, Texas, where they said we would be transferred into the army infantry. A person could have heard the moans and groans for miles. The air war in Europe was over and won, they claimed, and air superiority in the South Pacific already accomplished. Since we had been through air force basic training a few months earlier, the army only put us through three weeks of instruction, mainly to learn about grenade launchers, the M-1 and the Browning automatic rifle. I was rated a carbine expert. (Dad had banned firearms from our farm, and his ban helped me: I didn't have any bad habits to break.)

The army pumped live rounds over our heads and

exploded dynamite sticks as we tried snaking under the barbed wire and through sloppy mud. After one such grueling day our officer marched us off the training field and told us we better hurry in before the mess closed. To save time our hungry squad of twelve decided the quickest route to dinner was to shower with our rifles and field packs on. It seemed advantageous at first, but we hadn't realized the mud would plug the drain, the drain would overflow, the water would spill out the door, and a stream would run past the office of the commander who would ground us an entire weekend. Rifles weren't meant for water, he said, and they had to be stripped, oiled and cleaned before standing inspection. We never did that again!

After living with my dad for eighteen years, army discipline wasn't harsh, only an exciting diversion, invigorating, and action-packed. When my back hit the bunk at night I was so beat I didn't have any energy left to let my mind wander and to miss Minnesota.

The army then sent us home for a three-week furlough after which we were to head straight for Fort Meade, Maryland, and then off to fight Adolf Hitler in Germany. During my stay at home I visited Grandpa and Grandma Frederick, who were caring for my Great-Grandma Kramer by then. In German tradition the younger generation, my grandparents, were caring for the older. Knowing that Germany was my destination because I had told her, Grandma Kramer gave me her black address book, the one she had cherished since leaving Germany. It was filled with the addresses of relatives who might soon be shooting at me.

At Fort Meade the army herded us into a troop train, its black shades drawn. Since Baltimore was only ten miles east we were figuring on a half-hour train ride at best before having to board a troop ship for Europe. But our train chugged west instead, a surprise to all, and speculations on our ultimate destination ran wild. Every 3:00 a.m., in total darkness, nowhere near any town or farm, the engineer would stop the train to let us out for calisthenics. The mystery puzzled everyone. Five days after leaving Baltimore the train abruptly jerked to a halt in a rail yard near San Francisco. The army had purposely told us that Germany was our final destination in case our relatives were also spies. So far I had served the U.S. military in Minnesota, Colorado, Mississippi, Texas, Maryland and California and hadn't yet fought the enemy.

Our troop ship sailed underneath the Golden Gate Bridge as others and I waved good-bye to smiling civilians on shore. For many soldiers it would be their last glimpse of America. Our future, uncertain as it was then, would surely involve, we felt, shooting at the Japanese and/or being shot at on a South Pacific island.

Three thousand troops were stacked three high in the bulkheads, packed tighter than canned sardines. If the soldier above you were heavy, his butt would graze your hip when you turned over while trying to sleep. Sailing across a South Pacific summer was akin to taking a hot shower without an exhaust fan. Our farm had better smells. After two days the brushes on our cooling fans wore out and we had to steal replacement brushes to run them. A detour had to be made to Pearl Harbor because scarlet fever had broken out on board. Tension began building at facing the Japanese.

The sea near Pearl Harbor was especially rough — so much for the Pacific Ocean being calm — and nearly everyone felt sick from all the tossing and turning. After leaving behind twenty-five scarlet fever cases in Hawaii we sailed west as part of a different army convoy. The least objectionable "ride" was had in the ship's middle section, we learned, where we tried disguising our gnawing fear of war by playing cards. It was an army convoy on a navy ship and navy personnel were the ones responsible for manning the machine guns, rifles and five-inch cannon that would protect us in case of enemy attack. One day a sailor let fly with a giant red balloon off stern while other sailors took turns firing a machine gun and the five-inch gun at it as practice. Not one of them could shoot it down. After that we did not feel so secure.

Boom! I jerked my head around at the sound as a depth charge flew high into the air and splashed into the ocean.

Sonar had picked up a Japanese submarine. Our ship began zigzagging back and forth across the open sea, and because of the sighted sub we continued zigzagging for the next couple of days. The balmy weather and my own nervous perspiration combined to glue my clothing tight to the skin. As we disembarked in the Philippines, we had hoped for an overnight rest on land before being transported out the next day to our assignment. Instead they directly ordered us into a Landing Craft Mechanized (LCM) that chugged south towards the island of Mindanao.

"Frederick! You're with Company G, 34th Infantry, 24th Division." An officer also assigned me to a squad of twelve men and made me its first scout because I would be a smaller target for the enemy — I was short, he said — and an expert shot. I took the "point." The previous point man, who was going home, clued me in. The Japanese army on Mindanao was in bad shape, he said, because its supply and reinforcement lines had been cut. Our objective was to push them east across the island. Most of the Filipinos hated the Japanese and took great joy in betraying them. I had to be careful to not lead the squad around pockets of resistance because the Japanese could ambush us from the rear. They had to be confronted head-on and wiped out from every bunker, cave and building, and the weapons to do it with were hand grenades and flamethrowers.

Up ahead was a village. A Filipino local whispered to me that three Japanese were inside a straw hut. Being point man, I had to run to the hut and squat down underneath it without being heard. I didn't want to be on the receiving end of any firepower. My pounding heart felt like it would give me away. Any second they could open fire. I motioned for the squad and they ran up one by one until we had the hut surrounded. After one of us kicked the door in we opened fire to kill or be killed. It was a one-sided firefight. They were weakened from malaria and would have died from that anyway.

The rain pelted us each night in the steamy Mindanao jungle and when it cleared the next day the sun beat down unbearably upon our necks and helmets. Our fresh water hung inside twenty-gallon canvas bags. The only time we bathed was in a stream and not long after doing it spots began appearing all over our skin. The locals had used our bathing stream as an open sewer and we had what was called "jungle rot." When we faced no resistance we marched like crazed madmen, hacking away at the dense underbrush with machetes. Sometimes we ran ahead of supply and had to fill our canteens with rainwater gathered overnight from our ponchos. When enough rain didn't fall we gathered water from puddles on the ground and used iodine tablets to purify it, which made it taste bad, but at least the water was wet.

Meanwhile, over two months as first scout was taking its toll on my psyche. Even though I performed my job well, it was a very heavy burden to bear, what with being the first shot at and having to make snap judgments on enemy troop strength and having to relay the information up the chain of command. One stupid mistake and we were dead.

One day a call went out for volunteers. Normally a soldier didn't volunteer for anything but since I had the most dangerous job already, I thought, What could be worse? I raised my hand. They ordered me to headquarters where I was instructed to turn in my rifle for a sidearm and report for kitchen duty. I would be a cook — a very happy chef, indeed.

My first assignment as "third cook" was to scramble eggs for breakfast, which I did, mixing pounds and pounds of powdered eggs in with fifteen gallons of water. The mess sergeant commanded me to keep stirring the eggs lest they scorch. Next to me another cook was supposed to be mixing his coffee grounds into a thirty-gallon container of boiling water but instead he dumped them into my eggs by mistake. I kept stirring the eggs, being careful to obey the sergeant's order. When the sergeant saw the "seasoned" eggs, he told me to "skim off the coffee grounds as they float to the top, but don't take too much off or we won't have enough to feed the troops." As I began serving the food that morning, the sergeant made an impromptu announcement to the hungry troops: "Don't pepper the eggs today, the cook done it for you."

I enjoyed making the best of what the army called food.

One time I received a number of thirty-pound waxed cardboard boxes marked "STEAK." Inside was "stew" meat, packed by a meat company that had probably invoiced the army for real steak. The troops had been anticipating "the good stuff" and it was my job to make the best of the situation. But I couldn't turn stew meat into steak.

Not long after we had pushed the Japanese army on Mindanao into the ocean and while the plans were being drawn up for an all-out invasion of Japan, the atomic bomb fell August 6, 1945, on Hiroshima, Japan. The Japanese surrendered after a second one devastated another city, Nagasaki, days later. I'm certain the atomic bomb saved my life because I would have been in the first wave of

Hiroshima after the atomic bomb exploded overhead

troops to hit the Japanese coast, a wave that would have had a very high casualty rate.

Towards Japan we steamed as part of the occupation force, eventually disembarking at a former Japanese submarine base five miles off the coast of Hiroshima. The deserted Japanese barracks there seemed inviting because for a full year we had been sleeping in either tents or on cramped ship bunks. We rushed off the ship as a red sun was fading in the west, and later unrolling our sleeping bags inside the barracks. About 2:00 a.m. bedlam broke out. The barracks was crawling with lice. Medics squirted us with dusting powder as we stripped buck-naked on the commons area under an uncomfortably bright light. All our clothing had to be washed and sterilized.

In daylight we saw the island's defense system; it would

have been nearly impenetrable had we tried to invade it. They had booby-trapped the beach with tank traps, slit trenches and barbed wire. When war historians claimed one million Americans would have died invading Japan, I believe them. Imagine what would have happened if America were being invaded: every 3-year-old and up from Texas to Maine to Alaska would have been armed. The atomic bomb alone persuaded the Japanese to surrender.

We were the first American soldiers in Hiroshima. It was a skeleton, charred black, with the outer walls of a few reinforced concrete buildings left as an eerie monument to the destruction. Three days elapsed before we saw any Japanese citizens. They were wary at first because their government had told them we would kill all the men and children, and rape the women. They had a reason to be afraid: after all, we were soldiers from the same country that had nuked them three months earlier, killing 280,000 of their friends, relatives and neighbors. I did hire some Japanese citizens. It really didn't matter for what; the purpose was to get them working and to build trust between us.

A pleasant woman who spoke English was hired at our battalion office and said she had been jumping off a streetcar when the atomic bomb had exploded. The part of her body facing the blast was turning black from the radiation, and the part shielded from it wasn't. She eventually died. No one knew then that radiation would linger much after a nuclear blast. (Because of my exposure to atomic radiation I later joined the Atomic Veterans Association, which seeks government compensation for soldiers sickened by radiation. When my father died at 87 he had twice the hair I had at 44. The radiation also may have affected Rose's two miscarriages, both boys.)

On Thanksgiving Day, at Hiroshima, the navy delivered thirty frozen turkeys and my crew stayed up past 3:00 a.m. roasting them brown before setting them out on tables for the next day's feast. A few hours after I went to sleep the mess tent caught fire. I don't know how it happened. The soldiers on duty did right by quickly extinguishing it but in doing so they dressed the turkeys in powdery foam. Our mess sergeant saved the day by suggesting we peel off the skin and wash the naked birds clean. The feast went on as planned.

It wasn't long before I was asked to be the shift leader, at 19, to manage a six-man crew ranging in age from 18 to 34. Soon we were rated the best shift of all three. Having been prepared for it by years of managing five younger brothers while my parents were away, the task of managing six soldiers who generally followed orders seemed easy. It felt grand being the food king to 250 hungry men each day. And to think I was discovering my twin niches of cook and restaurant manager in this most unlikely of spots.

A few high-ranking officers tried splitting up my shift by proposing to disburse some of its members to poorer performing units, a move that would theoretically improve the other two shifts but destroy mine in the process. It broke my heart when they laid out their plan because I had worked so hard to get that shift going. I was sitting on a milk can filled with water at the time and as the anger shook through my body I jumped up and the can tipped over, off flew its top, and the cold water inside it splashed the officers who were making the proposal. "No way!" I yelled. I continued ranting for nearly five minutes. It was the first time in my life that I had ever lost control of my emotions. When I told my crew about the proposal to split us up they rebelled. Ultimately the officers did cave in and we remained intact.

I went from the frying pan and into even more radiation when our unit was ordered in June 1946 to Nagasaki, the other city devastated by the bomb. Thankfully I was stationed there only two months before earning enough points for home. Nagasaki seemed a mirror image of Hiroshima: a skeleton of a city, with only blackened walls of reinforced concrete buildings remaining, total devastation over a two-mile radius.

While sailing home on a navy ship in July 1946 I volunteered to help in its galley as a cook, which seemed peculiar to some sailors — volunteering, that is — but it beat tossing and turning on a cramped bunk below deck for two weeks. The first question out of my mouth after reporting for duty, as a volunteer was, Why do you have those railings around your stoves? They told me to wait and see. Not long thereafter, out on the open sea, the ship began rocking in concert with the ocean waves, the pots followed suit and slid across the stove and slammed into the containment rail. A moment later they clanked the other rail after the next wave. We never filled the pots more than two-thirds full.

At Fort Lewis, Washington, a Red Cross worker handed me a telegram from my parents that said Jerry, my brother, was also at the same Fort Lewis, preparing for the Japanese occupation force. Visiting him felt great. I hadn't hugged a family member in two years.

From there, following a train trip where I also worked as a volunteer cook, the army discharged me at Fort Sheridan, Illinois. Since the discharge placed me near Chicago, before going home I decided to look up a friend from Keesler Field, Lee Boeske. From what he said, I learned that he had ended up in Salt Lake City as a drummer in an air force band. To make extra money, he had flown home as often as possible to pick up a car from his father's Buick dealership in Chicago before driving it back to sell it at a good price to his buddies in Utah. It sure beat what I was doing. (Rose and I are still good friends with Lee and Dorothy.)

Sal with Lee Boeske

Five of the six older Frederick boys served in the U.S. military. (In due time, Eddie, the exception, became the chancellor at the University of Minnesota-Waseca.) As a veteran of the armed forces, I feel very strongly that all veterans should belong and be active in at least one of the veterans' organizations. Personally, I am a life member of the American Legion, VFW, DAV, Atomic Veterans, and the chaplain of American Legion Post 518 North Mankato, Minn.

Even though we desperately wanted it otherwise, all five Fredericks couldn't make it through their military service without being hit by the violent slings and arrows of war. Our family foundation was shaken May 6, 1953, when we received word that Nicky, my brother, had been killed in action in Korea.

Pvt. Nicholas J. Frederick
BORN: MAY 16, 1932
KILLED IN KOREA: MAY 6, 1953

The Saulpaugh

CHAPTER THREE

The newspaper ad read: "Cook Wanted at Saulpaugh Hotel."

Since all nine Frederick children couldn't live off one 260-acre farm, I felt I had to search for a job in Mankato, hopefully as an aviation mechanic, which had been my first love from air force training in Colorado and Mississippi. But in 1946, Mankato didn't have many aviation jobs. I was scanning the daily newspaper when my eyes dropped to an ad for a cook at the Blue Blazer, Mankato's finest restaurant, inside the Saulpaugh Hotel. That day, armed with the newspaper, I approached its chef, and soon I was rattling off my army cook and shift leader experience. I could tell he was sizing me up as I spoke.

"Forget it, kid," he said, "because working here is nothing like that." An uncomfortable pause later he snorted at me, and added, "I'm going to tell you two things: the first is, get the hell out of the business. The second is, if you stay in it, never, ever work for a club. With a club every member is your boss and no one needs that."

"Thank you, sir, for the advice. Do I have the job?" He said I could work a split shift, from 6:00 a.m. to 2:00 p.m. and 5:00 to 8:00 p.m. Since my home was ten miles away near Madison Lake — a distance that made a split shift impractical — he said I could live in the Saulpaugh Hotel in a back room that faced the railroad tracks. It was really not a rentable room. I couldn't sleep at all the first two weeks owing to the trains that rumbled by at all hours and to the leaky faucet. (That winter the inside window sill was so cold I used it as my "refrigerator.")

I applied for apprentice chef training in which the U.S. Government would pay the Saulpaugh Hotel to have Ray teach me the chef's trade. He put me through a rather unique initiation into the field: I had to hold a cold beer in my left hand, dunk the other hand into a gallon can of raw oysters, eat six oysters, one at a time, and chase them down with the beer. When I tried it, Ray complained I wasn't eating the oysters correctly, so he pulled one out and asked me to identify where its head was. How do I know? I answered. I had to swallow the head first, he said, or else the oyster might crawl back out.

Working at the Blue Blazer stimulated me so much I couldn't sleep very well at night. I had excess energy that needed burning. As a restless 20-year-old, I asked a bowling alley manager, Slim Wallrich, for a job setting pins by hand. He hired me for the 9:00 p.m. to 11:00 p.m. shift and to make double the money I would set two alleys at once by jumping back and forth over a partition. Sometimes a drunk released his ball down the alley just to laugh at my scrambling out the pit. Yes, I scrambled!

At the Blue Blazer I couldn't help noticing a beautiful girl who began sitting at the table nearest the kitchen door. Ray introduced me to her. She was Rosemary Kelly, who baby-sat Ray's children while he and his wife worked evenings.

Rose, Age 9

Ray had a wicked temper. One noon hour Alice, a waitress, mistakenly served the wrong order to a customer and in anger Ray threw a two-tine fork at her. The missile sailed over her head, careened off a refrigerator and flew back to knock off his tall chef's hat. Always the dictator, Ray ran his restaurant as if it were a battleground and his employees the enemy. He taught me how to mismanage a restaurant. Every day, flak from the war beset the Blue Blazer in the form of threats, blame, and making others look bad. And it wasn't flak from just Ray either, nearly every employee joined the kooky kitchen conflict, from the cooks, waitresses, and on down to the custodians. With a calmer head Ray could have doubled his crew's productivity. I rarely fought in the war but saw the daily casualties.

My eyes kept drifting towards Ray's baby-sitter until one night after work I gathered up enough courage to escort her home. She seemed so vivacious, exuberant, candid — an Irish gal. She told me what she thought whether I liked it or not. From an early age, she explained, she had cared for her younger siblings because her mother had worked. I think she liked my stability and work ethic; and I worked hard when I worked and yet was able to have fun afterwards. At one point the company that owned the Saulpaugh Hotel, the Arthur L. Roberts Co., offered me the chef's position at its hotel in Rice Lake, Wisconsin, and I told them no. I had marriage plans.

Rose's mother set the tone for our marriage: "Don't come home crying to me," she said weeks before the wedding, "because if you have an argument with Sal I know it's going to be your fault." Rose thought her mother liked me more than her. We married October 1, 1949, and rented a house on May Street from Grandma McNamara.

Wedding photo, 1949 (Willie and Wanda Frederick, Sal, Rose, Margaret and Lorin Kelly)

The job offer in Wisconsin made me think: If they thought I could be a good head chef, then why not become one? A promotion at the Saulpaugh Hotel would have to come at Ray's expense though, and since he was the boss that wasn't very likely. One afternoon in early 1950, I heard from a friend that the Topic Cafe needed a morning chef who could handle breakfast through late afternoon. On Jackson Street and near Mankato Teachers College, the Topic Cafe was a fast turnover place that served good food. After meeting with its owner, I was hired as "the kind of guy" he needed. Ray was disappointed but he understood. At least it wasn't a club, he said.

For the longest time the owner of the Topic Cafe, Frank, had wanted to visit his boyhood home in Tennessee and with my running the restaurant in his absence he could finally do it. After offering me a crash course in restaurant management, within a week he left for Tennessee. I did the best I could. His evening cook, Earl, took over for me late in the afternoon.

It didn't take me long to catch on that both Frank and Earl abused alcohol. Similar to the lessons Ray taught me with his mismanagement of the Blue Blazer, Frank's bumbles and grumbles taught me volumes in what not to do. At times I ran the cafe with Frank passed out drunk on a basement mattress. Sometimes Earl ruined the food I prepared for him. He smoked and drank and had lost his sense of taste because of it, and the result was an unwavering tendency to over season anything I prepared. I caught flak from customers for his mistakes.

In late 1951 Frank bought half a cow from a friend to make it through a meat shortage created by the Korean War. Frank tossed the cow into his Hudson, let it dangle out the trunk and as he drove along parts of it scraped the highway. Frank and his friend ultimately burped their way down the gravel alley behind the cafe and stumbled inside at 2:45 p.m., fifteen minutes before my shift was scheduled to end. They dragged the cow indoors. Frank asked me to cut it up, which I did, carefully picking out the stones, washing it, and finishing up at 6:00 p.m. I told Rose that evening that I was finished with Frank and his games.

It was time for a change. I became emboldened by the words of Frank's accountant who had asked me why I didn't own my own restaurant. He told me that Frank was making "$950 a month clear" even though he was running half the business out the door. Days later I was still chewing on the accountant's words when a prominent Mankato businessman, a regular, sat at the counter for his usual soup and sandwich special. Frank saw him and walked over. "Got what you like today, pea soup. I made it myself," he said to the businessman. "I'm going to give you a bowl for free and I want you to tell me how good it is." Frank set it in front of the businessman, who sipped the soup and said it tasted like dishwater. When the businessman pushed the bowl aside, Frank must have thought the soup would spill onto the floor because he jerked his hand out to catch it. In doing so it slopped all over his hand and burned it. In anger he slugged the businessman right off his stool. Within half an hour the businessman returned with a black eye and two policemen who hauled Frank away in handcuffs. News of the violent act spread fast. Weeks later, at the trial, a judge sentenced him to four weeks of business management training at what is now Minnesota State University. The training didn't seem to help.

    L. K. Petersen, Frank's accountant, told me that I was the glue holding the cafe together — Frank certainly wasn't much help — and once again he suggested that I buy my own place. Intrigued, I began peppering him with questions. He said he would return with answers in a few weeks and he did. He had found a place, he said, and had even worked on the financing for it. It wasn't as fancy as the Blue Blazer by any means, but rather the filthiest of filthy greasy spoons, the Hidden Inn, which could be bought for $3,000 plus elbow grease and was owned and operated by a one-armed man named Wimpy who had a metal hook in place of a hand.

    After buying it we shut down for five days to clean, wash and paint it into some semblance of respectability. At first the stove wouldn't disassemble because it was welded together from years of spilled grease. I wasn't worried about losing money because I had watched Ray and Frank "earn" profits while mismanaging a restaurant. If I worked hard I couldn't fail. Our main customers would be the 300 manufacturing employees who worked at the Automatic Electric plant directly behind the Hidden Inn. Walk-in traffic from the street barely existed. We were so off the beaten path, so tucked away in an obscure alleyway no wider than a door, so hidden, that only the most adventuresome soul could find us. If a customer met another in the alleyway they had to turn sideways to squeeze through. The Hidden Inn had two screen doors, a window in the back, a counter and two booths. It didn't take long for the police to realize that if they opened the back window and parked their police cruiser under it, they could sit inside and drink hot coffee and still hear the periodic barking of the police radio. When an emergency call erupted, they ran like crazy for their cruiser.

A former waitress and able teacher, Evie Fasnacht, taught Rose, and she picked up on it almost immediately. But there were days at the Hidden Inn that stretched Rose to her limits. Walt Comstock and Cal Peters walked in every day at 10:30 a.m. and expected me to put toast down in advance for them and for Rose to ready their tea. Walt ran a nearby gas station and Cal sold for Marigold Dairy. The toast and tea had to be in front of them by the time they reached the counter. One morning about 8:00, more than two hours before and Walt and Cal were to arrive, Rose accidentally tipped a bowl of hot oatmeal onto her hand. Dr. O. H. Jones, our family doctor, bandaged her up and ordered her home, which meant I had to cook and wait on customers the entire day. In sauntered Walt and Cal that day at 10:30 a.m., asking for Rose and their tea. I explained to them as best I could why she had been sent home. For whatever reason, they waved good-bye to me and left. At 11:00 a.m. the telephone rang and I could hardly keep it to my ear because of all the strident words rolling off Rose's tongue. Evidently Walt and Cal, after departing the Hidden Inn, had driven to my house and asked Rose to fix their daily toast and tea. She told them they had to serve themselves, which they did, boiling the water and buttering their own toast.

Another day "Mac" McGowan, the father of Jack McGowan, owner of McGowan Water Conditioning, waltzed in with a huge bump under his suit coat. An Irish smirk later he pulled out a pencil thirty inches long and slammed it onto the counter. He said that if he was going to write big orders, he needed "big equipment." We all exploded in laughter.

To speed up coffee hour we began self-service and the customers loved it. They could walk in, grab coffee, doughnuts, rolls and toast, lay their money down — and make their own change without having to wait. In a breadbox of a restaurant like ours that was the only way we could move people in and out in order to make room for the next group of hungry customers.

The price for a cup of hot coffee in Mankato was a nickel and not one restaurant in town made money at it. To fix it, literally, all the restaurateurs met one evening and agreed to raise the price of a cup of coffee to a dime beginning the next day. The customers couldn't protest too much, we figured, because all the restaurants would be charging it. When I opened the Hidden Inn the next morning, naturally, all my regular customers complained. I tried to apologize for and justify the increase. An hour later a guy who simply wouldn't take my "apology" told me he was "going down the street" where coffee was still a nickel. Indeed, the owner of a restaurant down the street had caved in. I immediately telephoned all the other restaurant owners and told them to send all their complaining customers to Mike's restaurant. They did, and he was so jammed up at noon with nickel coffee customers that he couldn't serve his regulars. In three days he jacked his price back up to a dime.

The Hidden Inn grossed $13,280 its first year. We needed every ounce of our youth to withstand the grueling seventy-two-hour work schedule. As the cafe matured and Rose became pregnant we hired a person to wash dishes. Finally, when it reached what we thought was its full potential, L. K. Petersen suggested that we buy another much bigger restaurant. We had an extra mouth to feed at home. Soon we would be feeding extra ones at work.

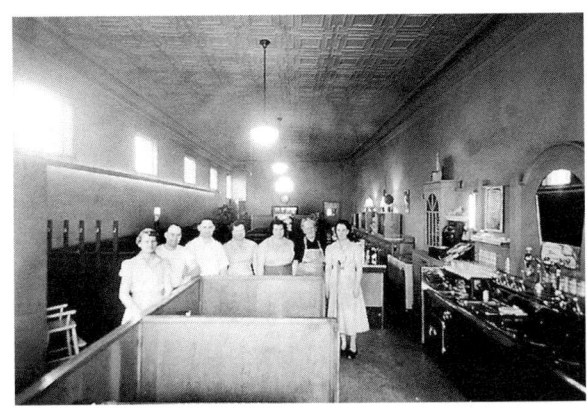

The Corner Cafe, 1954: Millie Otsea, Sal, Bob, Rosella Volk, Imelda Connor, Ella Gilmore, Thelma Rohloff

CHAPTER FOUR

The owner of the Corner Cafe should have retired three years earlier but had held out in the hope that his sons would run the business after returning from Korea. When they returned home, they didn't want any part of it. So we inherited their employees and the entire eighty-seat cafe for $7,500, a good price for a good location, directly across the street from the Stahl Hotel. At the closing Bob and I signed away everything we owned to the bank.

Since I couldn't manage both cafes, I had asked my brother Bob, who had been discharged from service in the Korean War and trained as a baker, if he would consider going into business with me. The timing couldn't have been worse for them, though. He and his wife, Anne, had just moved into a new home in South St. Paul where he was working for Swift. In our discussions he indicated that he really would like to accept my offer but he didn't know if he could persuade Anne. He eventually did, and they sold their home and moved into a basement apartment on Mound Avenue in Mankato.

We struggled through a few confusing telephone calls at first because both of us had been nicknamed "Freddie" in the service. To keep confusion to a minimum when telephone calls for "him" rang, we took on the names "Sal" and "Bob" in all our advertising as well as with any correspondence with friends and relatives. It took only a short time before most Mankatoans began using the new monikers. (Having five nicknames over a lifetime is an advantage when you're at a party and can't remember who's talking to you. You just have to wait until they say one of the nicknames. It helps jog the memory.)

In 1954 the Corner Cafe had three 100-watt bulbs staring down from the ceiling and a behemoth three-ton air conditioning unit, the only one of its breed in town — and very costly to run — that could barely cool a ninety-degree day down to eighty. We alternated shifts. I worked alongside Anne while Bob stayed home with their kids, then Rose began a shift with Bob while I baby-sat ours. We continued living like this for five years until another of life's sudden events ultimately changed our lives for the better.

One weekend in 1959, VFW members began pouring into Mankato for their annual state convention. They hung from our canvas awning out front. They picked up our tables and danced with them and carried the tables over their heads. They partied day and night. I heard this banging noise and I ran over to the basement stairs to see what it was. Directly below me, and stumbling up from the basement in a stupor, was this drunken individual carrying the porcelain tank top to my basement toilet. I asked him where he was headed and he yelled back: "When I get up there you'll find out!" I told him he wasn't going anywhere with my tank top. "Are you big enough to stop me?" I told him I wasn't, but that the police were and they would. Anne had already dialed for the police who arrived within minutes and forced the drunk to reinstall the tank top. Bob and I didn't leave the restaurant for twenty-six hours straight for fear of it being destroyed. Afterwards we began discussing the possibility of getting out of the restaurant business.

The hours were long and the facility was antiquated. Bob and I called L.K. Petersen to see if he could help. He advised us to stay in the business — and in the same spot too, because it was a great location — but to remodel in the hope it would also upgrade the clientele. Amazingly, he had already chatted over our situation with three food service equipment companies and all three said that the next new or greatly remodeled restaurant in Mankato would have customers standing in line outside. A new restaurant hadn't been built or an old one remodeled for fifteen years and many Mankatoans were driving thirty miles to New Ulm for a good meal. Our choices were clear: either get bigger and better or get out of it.

All three equipment companies urged a remodel and the president of our bank, Erv Kurth, agreed to finance it. Clem Scheurer, the building owner, said he would pour a new sidewalk, lay a new roof and improve the storefront. Momentum seemed to be gathering to stay in business and remodel — and that was exactly what we did. For an equipment company we chose Palm Brothers, the highest priced company but the best. On our own we visited restaurants in Iowa that had been remodeled by them, and they were all thriving and visually appealing units. When their representative, Jack Watson, offered a detailed drawing of their proposal we were speechless: the change would be drastic. They replaced the floor, ceiling, walls, wiring, plumbing and air conditioning system, and took away eight seats, from eighty to seventy-two, when Jack brought the kitchen grills and fryers into the middle of the room. Before the remodel, I was sixty feet from the front door but after it only twenty feet away, where I could keep my eyes on everything.

The night before the new "Frederick's Cafe" debuted, our families and our employees' families staged a party there in part to try out the new equipment. When my dad strolled in that evening he ran his eyes over all the stainless steel and quipped, "How in the hell can you brothers get two hundred and sixty acres into a twenty by sixty space?" It happened exactly the way Palm Brothers said it would. Business tripled overnight and on weekends they were waiting in line to get in. Our customers appreciated the upscale remodel and the revised menu, and the employees adored the better working conditions. We now stole business from New Ulm.

Palm Brothers had expertise in areas we knew little about, and they helped develop a menu that fit the equipment. "Pete" Petersen helped price the food. The remodel altered everything. Suddenly we were out front with the customers where I could laugh and talk alongside them. Customers watching me flip pancakes as they walked in yelled, "How's the happy chef today?" While I was heading towards the bank one evening, a man shouted at me from his car, "Hey, happy chef!" If I was late to a community meeting, a moderator might say, "We can start now, the happy chef is here!" To capitalize on the nickname, we asked Bob Muellerleile, of M&M Signs, to blow a neon sign of a jumping "happy chef" that clicked its heels and waved a spoon. He did and it was an interesting concept.

But I wasn't happy with the clubs. The first seeds of political involvement were planted in me when I found out, in the early '60s, that the local "clubs" in Mankato were selling liquor to anyone that asked for it, even 17-year-olds, and they were advertising to the general public when the state law was specific that only members and their guests could be solicited. The clubs, such as the American Legion, VFW and others, were being operated as regular restaurants. I phoned "Sarge" Carstensen, a mover and shaker in the American Legion, to complain to him. I called City Council members. The future of our local restaurant industry was being put in jeopardy and I wasn't going to let them win. Not long thereafter, the City Council met with the clubs and, in essence, asked them to stop breaking the law. My business philosophy always has been this: if you don't keep moving your competitors will run right over you.

A few years later with Frederick's Cafe, Brett's Grill and the Newman Center – the latter two we began managing — it seemed we were just treading water again, headed nowhere in downtown Mankato in an industry that had begun building restaurants on conspicuous highway sites. Bob and I added brother Tom to the team, and now we had three families to feed. Palm Brothers proposed a plan for us to build a restaurant on U.S. 169. We had to keep moving.

In early 1962, an individual pressured us to build a new restaurant on U.S. 169 near Minneopa Park, southwest of Mankato. Palm Brothers said that it was a horrible location and we agreed. Most Mankato traffic went north towards Minneapolis and we would miss that business if we relocated near Minneopa Park. Also, from Minneapolis, Mankato was a stop for travelers and a restaurant five miles south of town would lose potential business, too.

Logic seemed to dictate that we search for land north of town, and indeed we settled on a spot just north of Mankato city limits, a couple of hundred yards west of the Minnesota River. But could the sandy soil there support a heavy building? Soil borings forty-five feet deep indicated we had found the old riverbed. Even though a foundation for a restaurant on that spot would have to rest on sand, we felt we had to make it work somehow because that site was nearly perfect. It was the first open space driving into Mankato from the north. The first Happy Chef was built on a bed of compacted clay and girdled with forty 55-gallon barrels of tar that resisted flood pressure. (We've had three floods reach near the front door in thirty-five-years there and not a droplet has ever touched the basement. The local health inspector shakes his head in disbelief at the building's watertight strength during a flood.)

Rather than recycle the Frederick's Cafe name, Rose suggested naming the new 180-seat restaurant "Happy Chef." The brothers agreed to the descriptive, upbeat name.

All my brothers had an equal share in the business, starting with Bob, and then Tom, who had helped at the Hidden Inn and Frederick's Cafe while attending college. The reason for giving them equal shares was logical: I couldn't predict when customers would arrive. As an equal owner, when one of my brothers telephoned to my home to say three busses had just pulled in, I'd go help them. In an unequal partnership, the lesser partner wouldn't nearly be as willing to make those personal sacrifices.

All three of us filled roles. I was the front man and visionary, active in the chamber of commerce, mediator between the brothers, and who managed the North Mankato unit into the '70s. Bob was the maintenance man, who was tight with suppliers, plumbers and electricians. Tom, who had served with the U.S. Army Justice Department, was the legal advisor and financial man. As we evolved, we added brother Bill as an equal partner and eventually he became the personnel manager.

Bill shouldered a heavy weight from the beginning when he agreed to manage our new second unit in Winona, Minn. We had to know if we could operate a unit outside Mankato. After Winona succeeded, we opened Owatonna, Minn., and Story City, Iowa, which was our test market for out-of-state expansion. Story City added new challenges: could we adapt to new health regulations, tax rates, state laws, and a work ethic? To be a good neighbor in each new city we tried to buy most of our supplies from local vendors.

It was a combination of many things that enabled Happy Chef to grow to over fifty restaurants — among them, cooperation from suppliers, and dedicated and loyal employees. Teamwork was our core value.

*Speaking in Japan for the National
Restaurant Association, 1979*

CHAPTER FIVE

Even when Happy Chef had only one location I realized the need for an organization like the Minnesota Restaurant Association (MRA) that brought restaurant owners under one big tent. There was strength in numbers. I worked on the MRA board and was named its president on January 1, 1968.

Not quite three months later, on March 31, I was reattaching a rain gutter to my home when the telephone rang. A caller bore sad news: MRA's executive director had died of a heart attack. He had been the only person knowledgeable about our finances and the sole owner of our annual trade show. No one knew quite what to do, but since I was the president, the task of "doing" something fell on me. The next six months would be the worst of my life; the rain gutter would remain unattached for six more years.

Happy Chef was aggressively adding units, MRA was floundering, and I was splitting my time between the two, averaging three days a week in the Twin Cities holding MRA together when I should have been building Happy Chef. That's when my brothers really moved to the forefront. We had meetings, made our decisions and if I had to be at MRA they got the job done without me. Even during the darkest of days I could always see the light at the end of the tunnel.

To protect MRA from hemorrhaging in the future, its board, along with Earl Jorgenson, president of the state hotel association, and Dutch Cragun, president of the state resort association, formed an umbrella organization and hired a director to oversee all three organizations and to manage the trade show. Each group maintained its own identity and name. The umbrella organization was named the Upper Midwest Hospitality Association. I stayed on for two years as president of MRA and seven more as a board member to finish what I had started. From that moment on, the Minnesota Restaurant Association, under the Upper Midwest Hospitality Association, increased in membership over the years from 400 to 4,000 today. I am deeply proud of the new organization.

In 1971 the National Restaurant Association (NRA)

asked me to join its board, the most prestigious in the industry, and to represent its membership in the Dakotas and Minnesota. Restaurant owners needed a lobbyist organization to inform Congress of industry issues. Even though my volunteer service on the board cost me nearly $6,000 a year in personal travel and lodging expenses, I could easily justify the cost and time spent because the work ultimately benefited not only Happy Chef, but also the industry. The board met three times a year in different parts of the country, about four days each time, and I served the maximum three terms, nine years in all, through 1980. My brothers tolerated my absence because I was able to complete all my necessary Happy Chef duties. (Unlike so many executives, I wasn't tied to a time-consuming hobby that could distract me from my work duties. Work was my "hobby.")

In 1972 I was named to the Hennessey Evaluation Team, the NRA's annual present to the air force that evaluated the quality of some of their dining halls. The morning I was to fly out from Mankato I almost missed the plane. A snowstorm had hit the night before and I had neglected to figure in a longer driving time from my home to the airport. The airline knew I was trying to get there, but it couldn't wait forever. I boarded as they were closing up the plane for take-off. It was an ominous start to a world tour that would end in like fashion.

Two Air Force captains involved in food service escorted me around the world and through ten dining halls in a thirty-four day period. From Minneapolis I flew to orientation in Philadelphia, after which the captains and I flew a commercial airliner from LaGuardia to Germany. From there we visited bases in Turkey, Greece, Italy, Spain, and two bases in Taiwan — one of which monitored Mainland China from a mountaintop. Then we flew to a base in Oregon, to California, Texas, Alabama, Arizona, and finally to the U.S. Air Force Academy in Colorado Springs. It was fun wearing the star of a brigadier general, albeit for a short time. Our Hennessey Evaluation Team set four records that year: the youngest team ever (average age 45), most days traveled (34), most miles traveled (50,000) and most bases evaluated (10).

Never fly a Turkish airline. In Turkey, the U.S. Air Force instructed us to stand by the gate an hour before take-off and make a mad dash for the plane when the gate opened. The airline was first-come, first-served, with all the slowest runners left behind. When the gate finally opened, my traveling companions were away so it was up to me to run to the plane with all the other "potential" passengers nipping at my heels. I wrestled up the stairway, wormed in and saved two seats. When the plane was ready for take-off, a few of the people that had lost the mad dash for seats refused to leave, standing firm in the aisle. Soldiers were summoned, and one of them clubbed a passenger and blood from the wound spattered my jacket. Never fly Air Italia either. Our pilot must have been a former fighter pilot. Soon after take-off the stewardess walked the aisle carrying but one cup of coffee at a time and we figured out why when the pilot began making sharp turns in the rough air, a few passengers screamed bloody murder, and luggage became leather missiles that littered the aisles.

On the final leg from New York to Chicago, our Delta pilot announced that he might have to land the plane on its belly because his landing gear didn't seem like it was fully locking. He spun circles around O'Hare for forty-five minutes, giving the control tower a good view in the hope they could visually inspect it. In desperation, the flight engineer wiggled through a floor opening, and he determined that the landing gear was "probably" locked. We were ordered into crash position while the pilot attempted to land into a sea of foam sprayed from an armada of firefighting equipment. After the first bump the landing gear held and we veered into the grass. An airline worker ran up to insert locking pins into the landing gear as we stopped.

It was a once-in-a-lifetime trip in which the air force literally rolled out the red carpet all along the way. Using information our team provided, they began serving fast food, in addition to regular cafeteria food, at all its dining halls. Many newer airmen appreciated the fast food because it helped them make an easier transition to military life.

We ate with airmen, scrutinized their kitchens, and monitored menu, food taste and general procedures.

At a dining hall in Europe, 4:30 in the morning, I watched as an airman poured a whitish substance into a coffee urn. I introduced myself to him, and explained that in all my years in the food industry I had never poured anything like that into coffee. He said it was salt and that he was doing it on purpose. "I'm a line mechanic, not a damned cook," he said. His actions went into my report.

In 1979, the Japan Foodservice Association invited the five chairmen of the key committees of the NRA to a two-week tour of Japan. As chairman of the Education Committee my colleagues and I participated in eight seminars in eight different cities on a variety of foodservice subjects. It was a real learning experience, both culturally and professionally, for both associations. Rose and I marveled at the comfort and speed of the bullet trains, the hydrofoil boats and the well-maintained and clean taxis, but by the end of the trip we were looking forward to sinking our teeth into a good ol' American cheeseburger. Raw fish and plain white rice is not our favorite meal.

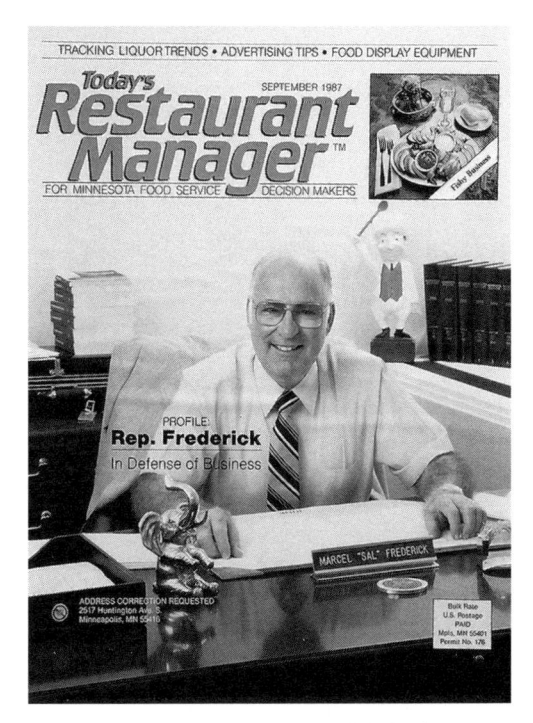

*September 1987 cover of Today's
Restaurant Manager magazine*

CHAPTER SIX

The recipe for Happy Chef's success mixed hard work with common sense. We picked menu items only after consulting with suppliers, who were substantial enough to have a diverse clientele from all over and savvy enough to be in tune with what people were eating. They wanted Happy Chef to succeed as much as we did. To keep in step with industry trends, I read trade magazines, attended NRA and MRA seminars and, like the Indian tracker, kept my ears low to the ground and ate out whenever I could. Sometimes Rose and I asked a competing restaurant manager for a complimentary menu and more often than not he supplied us with one.

We adopted or invented taste combinations. For my own personal taste, I discovered that a dollop of French dressing enhanced cottage cheese and that a little maple syrup improved corn beef hash. If not careful, a cook can overdue flavor enhancers and obscure the primary taste. My friend from Chicago, Lee Boeske, invented what he thought was a "winner" when he lightly coated one of his hamburger bun halves with peanut butter before inserting the beef. He thought the combination tasted great and wrote me a lengthy letter telling me so. Rose and I tried his, uh, creation, and as much as Rose likes peanut butter, it didn't flip her switch. Needless to say, his peanut buttery suggestion didn't make the Happy Chef menu. All new menu ideas had to pass muster with all the Frederick brothers.

Customers provided menu ideas. Many tried describing a food item from another restaurant as best as they could, yet without knowing how the restaurant had prepared it. From these often-sketchy descriptions we tried to concoct the alleged ambrosia ourselves.

Happy Chef was the first restaurant in southern Minnesota to leave its coffee pots on the tables so customers wouldn't have to keep asking for refills. Pleasing the customer was our primary concern for doing it — and as an added benefit we discovered it turned tables faster. Keeping our restaurants open twenty-four hours a day and offering breakfast anytime were also unique to our region.

I learned from taking a vacation that not everyone woke for breakfast at 5:00 a.m., and that most people sleep in and might enjoy eating breakfast later in the day.

A restaurant that desires success must respond to customer complaints. A Corner Cafe customer once complained about the taste of my potato salad. "How could he?" I said to the waitress. "I just made it." I tasted it before walking out to meet him and it seemed fine. "I understand you have a different idea about how potato salad should taste?"

He said: "It's good, but not as good as my mother's. She put ham in hers." We had a warm conversation about the taste sensation that was his mother's potato salad and after he left I diced ham and mixed some into a sample bowl. He was right: ham did improve potato salad, but adding it to our recipe would have necessitated a hefty rise in our selling price for it — and furthermore, Minnesotans not used to it might not have accepted it.

After we opened the first Happy Chef some people complained about the taste of our coffee. Hearing one too many complaint I began asking customers where they were raised and nearly all of them were from the South where chicory, a bitter herb, was added to coffee. Minnesota coffee was very mild. Complaints about service or bathroom cleanliness spiked during busier hours and when an employee hadn't shown up for an appointed shift and another had to do the work of two. (As Happy Chef consultants, Rose and I inspect both restrooms upon entering a restaurant and if they aren't up to standard I ask the manager to sanitize them right away.)

When searching for new sites for a restaurant we tried to detour around large population areas. The work ethic in big cities was inferior to that in most rural areas. Many big city employees worked at half-speed, it seemed, and wouldn't always respect authority. We tried a few Happy Chef units in metropolitan areas, but couldn't seem to mold the crew into our customary, cohesive work force. I can only speculate as to reasons why; either the employees there came from negative family environments or else they hadn't acquired the necessary character in life.

We decided to build a unit on a major highway in Plymouth, a Twin Cities suburb. Construction had already begun when the city planning commission's signing committee requested our presence. After literally dozens of these meetings they voted to ban that restaurant's outside statue because of its large size and a few meetings after that they objected to our on-building signs and a few meetings later they decided we had to plant evergreens and grass on the highway curb. (Of course, the trees and grass both died the next spring from salt poisoning, as I had predicted.) After we opened, the planning commission in Plymouth took away the direct turn into our parking lot and forced our customers to drive two-thirds of the way down the block before making a U-turn to head back towards us. A couple months later they let a fast food restaurant build next door and its drive-thru window traffic blocked our parking lot entrance during rush hour.

I argued with the planning commission over the drive-thru window because we simply couldn't operate profitably with our parking lot entrance blocked every noon. At one of my thirty-two meetings with them I showed them color photos of the traffic backup. I asked the committee chairman to monitor the backup for himself, and he did, agreeing with me but not knowing how to fix it. At the next planning commission meeting he asked me why us "fast food people" wanted to be in Plymouth anyway. Apparently he couldn't tell the difference between a Happy Chef and a McDonald's. We eventually sold what had been by all outward appearances, at least initially, a perfect Happy Chef location.

Another lesson that led to the withdrawal of our restaurants from large population areas was a lesson learned the hard way. We were almost finished with building our Edina unit when a building inspector, who had been in on the entire building process, shut us down the night before the advertised grand opening. We had to paint the walls behind all the kitchen equipment, he said, even though in opening any of our other units we had never been asked to paint that particular area of the wall. A restaurant like ours had all its stainless steel kitchen equipment permanently bolted in. Quickly, we had a contractor unbolt the equipment. At the next MRA meeting I told the strange story of having to unbolt equipment and paint walls to my fellow board members and they all laughed. I could have fixed the problem by paying off the inspector, they explained. I didn't operate that way, I said, to which a board member replied: "If you're going to operate in the big city, you better get used to it."

In the '90s a labor shortage challenged Happy Chef's growth and service level. Employees began missing more shifts versus twenty years earlier, a fact I attributed to a business climate where the employer seemed to need the employee rather than the other way around. In the '90s when an employee was fired, many didn't appear to be that upset because they knew the restaurant next door would hire them even with their poor work record — and many did, and with a bonus. Businesses were desperate for workers. Before I retired, restaurants jobs were less plentiful and employees held onto them.

Judging the work ethic of 2000 with that of the '60s, honestly, is like comparing a Yugo to a Cadillac — it is no comparison, even though Minnesota has a work ethic better than that found in most other states. In the '60s, parents brought their teenagers in and asked me to "do something with them. I don't care if you don't pay them, just work them." And they worked hard. Of course, I always paid them.

Another incident put the nail in the Edina unit's coffin. Friday at lunch rush I was helping the manager when a female employee said she would be leaving at 1:00 p.m., a full two hours before her shift was scheduled to end. I let her go because business was unusually light. The following Monday she didn't show for work and Tuesday the manager received a notice saying she had filed for unemployment. How could she be unemployed when she hadn't been laid off? On Friday when she strolled in to pick up her check, I asked her why she had filed. She said she worked at a business only long enough to become eligible for unemployment, and then would take a vacation, and when benefits ran out she would begin the cycle all over.

"Doesn't everybody do that?" she shrugged. I called the state unemployment division and they said she was within the letter of the law.

At Plymouth I walked in and found the restaurant dead empty in early afternoon when at least a few customers should have been there drinking coffee. I watched a customer walk in after me. Three waitresses and the assistant manager all ignored him while they were all busy yapping with each other. So the president of Happy Chef wedged his way in between their conversation and motioned them towards the waiting customer. Still they wouldn't budge. I said, "Somebody get that guy at the counter!" One of the waitresses snorted back, "you ain't telling me how to do my job" before she marched out the door. We sold Edina and Plymouth and never entered a metropolitan area again.

We tried to treat employees the same as members of our own family by respecting them as people, learning of any particular family situations that required special scheduling, if any, and then scheduling the crew around them. But we also had to keep our personal distance. To become entangled in an employee's personal affairs meant crossing over the line that most successful employers never touch.

An employee treated well was a happy employee, which meant they were more likely to attain a higher level of customer service. We tried but we couldn't achieve our goal of a big happy family at every unit. Our turnover rate was much lower than the industry average of 300 percent. One way we kept turnover low was in offering health insurance and a profit sharing plan — and we were one of the first chains to do it.

In planning a new restaurant we tried smoothing out any design flaws apparent in previously built units. To a customer then, a new Happy Chef might look like an older one, but an insider would notice details such as the piece of kitchen equipment moved a few inches to increase back room efficiency. Employees contributed to the tweaking process with their suggestions.

The microwave oven revolutionized the restaurant industry and its use early on helped us tremendously. Bob bought one off the floor at a '70s trade show. We couldn't find a spot for it at our North Mankato unit at first, so we set it on top of the office safe. Today I don't know how a restaurant could operate without one because it speeds cooking and lowers electric bills. Its one drawback is in not being able to crisp food, but microwave manufacturers will solve that.

We made the best of trying situations. In the late '60s we heard that a new U.S. 14 highway would pass near our North Mankato restaurant, so we decided to add a banquet facility in anticipation of it. When U.S. 14 construction didn't commence for years and our banquet hall sat empty we had to figure out a way to fill it. Our solution: a buffet. Every sports team for miles around began stopping in, busloads of athletes — nine busloads once — for our all-you-can-eat buffet. A few customers packed their lunch shrimp into their purses for a free dinner later at home. A buffet meant a higher food cost, but given our predicament we felt we had to try something.

Our famous Happy Chef statue didn't make our food taste any better or increase our level of service, but it sure brought thousands of people in. What a marketing tool. The first one received national press attention — too much attention apparently, because the city councils of a few cities passed ordinances that outlawed signs like ours. We became so concerned about community opinion near our North Mankato unit that we surveyed our customers about whether we should tear it down. Ninety-two percent said "keep it" and as a result the North Mankato statue stands yet today. Tens of thousands of photographs have been snapped of it and countless thousands of school children have sat on it. Mankato radio personality Henry Busse Jr. was its voice. When we had to remove a statue we tried to donate it to a nonprofit organization. One of them, altered to mimic a baseball umpire, sits today in a ballpark; another is a huge clown.

Many years ago we recognized the need for a full-time marketing person on staff and for it chose Jim Ulman, who had worked his way up from an entry level position as a high school junior to a manager. In the restaurant industry competitors stole marketing ideas from each other and adapted them to fit their own situations. Jim was tuned into the marketing schemes of other restaurant chains and he was able to react quickly.

Before his promotion to marketing, Jim managed a unit near Omaha, Nebraska, where he smoked cigarettes habitually. (I've never smoked.) At an awards dinner for Jim and others, right before introducing him, I lit an entire pack of cigarettes and walked around the dining room while grinding all the butts, one by one, into ashtrays. The awards group was in stitches. Even though I hadn't used his name in my introduction, everybody understood that I was making fun of Jim and his habit. Deeply embarrassed by the incident, he tried to quit smoking thereafter, eventually succeeding.

Experts that led management seminars I attended believed ten percent of any company's management ought to be "outside" hires to stimulate "outside-the-box" thinking inside the business. At Happy Chef, we never set quotas for outside hires; the ten percent happened naturally.

I wanted managers who worked until a job was finished. Ones who worked by the clock weren't well suited for it. If they were good managers they maintained a normal home life and the not-so-good ones, who couldn't properly manage, hire or train, had to work that much harder which resulted in a not-so-normal home life. Good workers, we learned, didn't necessarily make good managers, so we initiated an Assistant Managers Program from which we sifted out the best for promotion. I had trouble sometimes persuading assistant managers from Iowa to relocate to anywhere in Minnesota because of Minnesota's higher taxes. That was one of many anti-business situations existing in Minnesota.

Managers were trained to shake every employee's hand before a shift and ask him or her how they were doing. Besides being a simple act of respect, the handshake was done to learn if an employee was too distracted by an event in their personal life. If they were, a manager could send them home once a replacement arrived.

Our employees built the business. Our success as owners was to hire people who believed in us, honestly liked us, and shared our work ethic. Tom, my brother, has done an admirable job carrying the torch. Many of the people I hired are still with Happy Chef and over the years many of them have thanked me for hiring them. A few past employees have told me at one time they felt I had been too hard on them and it wasn't until years later, after they had become a success on their own, that they realized our high standards had helped them. In 1999, an article about me in the Mankato *Free Press* prompted a number of my former employees to write letters that warmed my heart. I gave them a chance to succeed, one writer explained. Another said they learned from me that if they worked hard enough their efforts would always be rewarded, either through wages, benefits or promotion.

I could be tough on a sloppy manager. After I returned from inspecting a Kansas unit, Tom asked me "what was going on down there." Egg usage was way too high, he said. I hadn't noticed any unusual breakfast activity so I immediately telephoned the manager who didn't seem to have a clue of what could be wrong. To figure it out myself I flew back down to Kansas, drove to the restaurant and, with a newspaper blocking my face, walked up to the counter. Within a half hour I heard a scraping noise coming from the back room. I peeked out from behind my newspaper and saw a case of eggs sliding across the back room floor, pushed along by a worker's foot. I heard the back door creak and I watched a young man drag the eggs outside. Playing detective, I went out the front and around back where I saw two employees tossing eggs at cars traveling up the freeway ramp.

I telephoned the manager at his home and he arrived within minutes to catch them in the act. He was angry — he had to be, I was with him — but despite my urgings he refused to fire them on the spot because, he said, he didn't have enough workers to fill in for them that night. I wasn't sympathetic at all to his plight because he was more than capable of working their jobs that night when factoring in my offer of help. After further discussion, the employees were fired. Needless to say that manager didn't cut it with Happy Chef.

* * *

A surprise came in early spring 1998 when South Central Technical College, Mankato, informed me that I would receive, at their upcoming graduation ceremonies, an honorary associate of applied science degree in culinary arts. I felt very humbled being in the presence of the administration and graduates.

In late 1999, as a crowning jewel to my career, the Minnesota Hospitality Hall of Fame, which honors active hospitality industry members with more than fifty years experience, inducted me as a member. Even though Happy Chef had been a chain of fifty restaurants when I sold my share and I was a consultant for ten years after that, the idea of being inducted had never crossed my mind.

A few people who tried to run a restaurant, and who didn't know how difficult the industry could be, have said we made the restaurant business look too easy. Years ago, an entrepreneur converted the Northern States building in Mankato into a restaurant and after it failed a group of Mankato businessmen invested $10,000 each to resurrect it. "The Phoenix" lasted a few months. One of my brother Bob's golf friends, a Phoenix investor, told Bob that we had cost him $10,000. "You Fredericks made the restaurant business look so easy I thought all you had to do was open the door and go to the bank."

I had but two regrets: the first was opening ten new restaurants in 1979. The National Restaurant Association had urged us to build them because the forecasted rush towards restaurants like ours would be amazing, they claimed. Anybody in their right mind should have known a chain our size couldn't grow ten restaurants in one year without experiencing staffing problems. Apparently we weren't in our right minds. The average new Happy Chef required a minimum of thirty-five employees to open, which meant ten new restaurants needed 350 new employees — and that meant 350 new employees that needed training and ten new managers to train them. Somehow we stumbled through the darkness of that year and learned a lesson in doing it.

The other regret was in not partnering with Super 8

motels. TraveLodge had wanted to build a motel on land we owned next to our North Mankato unit. That made us think: If TraveLodge thought our land was good enough, why not build a motel ourselves? After their five-year option expired, we met with the owners of Super 8, which was a small motel chain then in its infancy. Their work ethic and temperament matched ours perfectly. I attended several NRA seminars that included motel management — a mistake, because if Tom and Bob had joined me we would have bought into the motel industry as partners with the founders of Super 8. The people that ran the seminar said, "If you're a successful restaurateur you can run a motel with one hand tied behind your back." Each Happy Chef could have had a Super 8. My brothers decided to stay with what they knew best, which was Happy Chef, and I let them talk me out of it. It was an opportunity we should have grabbed onto with both hands and not let go. It was my fault for not making it possible for them to attend the seminars.

We did buy one franchise — one of the first Super 8s issued in the U.S. — and built it next door to the Happy Chef in North Mankato. The older Frederick brothers have been gradually selling out their portion of it to the younger brothers. My regret is we could have invested in Super 8 at ground level, been full partners, and sold out a few years ago along with the founders for millions and millions. It was a missed opportunity.

Sal with former President Gerald Ford.

Sal shaking hands with Vice-President George Bush.

Sal and Rose with Marilyn and Dan Quayle.

Rep. Gil Gutknecht, Rose, the late Rep. Sonny Bono and Sal.

Rose and Sal with Gen. Alexander Haig, 1983.

Rose and Sal with Tom Brokaw, 1988.

Vern Gagne being "choked" by Rose at Grandview Lodge, 1991.

Sal and Debbie Reynolds in Las Vegas, 1997.

Sal and Rose with their first great-grandchild, T.J. Swartout, 2000.

Wanda and William Frederick family, 1997 (Bob, Bill, Pat, Jerry, Sal, Tom, Helen, Ed).

Rose, Sal and daughters (L to R: Becky, Kathi, Rose, Vicky, Molly, Sal, Peggy, Mary).

"The Three Musketeers": Sal, Bob Foley, "Bill" Armstrong in 1944.

Wanda and Willie Frederick, Sal's parents.

50 years of marriage, 1949-1999.

Sal in Hawaii, 1999, for his 50th wedding anniversary.

Re-elect "Sal" FREDERICK

State Representative - 24B

Community Leadership
- Founder and retired president of a family business
- Past President Mankato Area Chamber of Commerce
- Past President Minnesota Restaurant Association
- Past President and 20 year member of Mankato Rehabilitation Center Board of Directors
- Past member of Mankato Township's Planning Commission
- Immanuel-St. Joseph's Hospital Development Committee
- Usher Captain St. John's Catholic Church
- Legion of Honor -- Catholic Order of Foresters
- South Central Senior Citizens Federation member
- American Association of Retired Persons member
- Minnesota Association for Crime Victims (LIfe Member)
- National Rifle Association member
- 8-year service in Minnesota House of Representatives

Veteran Duty
- Battle Star from Pacific Theatre World War II
- Life member of the American Legion, the VFW, Atomic Veterans, and Disabled American Veterans
- Serves on House of Representatives Veterans Committee

Education Involvement
- Born and raised on family farm near Madison Lake
- Graduated from Mankato area schools
- Mankato Technical College Advisory Committee member
- District 77 Alternative High School Advisory Committee
- MSU Community Campaign General Chair 1984
- Past Chair of Education Committee National Restaurant Association
- Former Ranking IR member of the State Legislature House Education Committee -- Higher Education Division
- Past Board member, MN Academic Excellence Foundation

CHAPTER SEVEN

In early 1984 a "search committee" from the Blue Earth County Republicans urged me to run for the state representative seat that retiring Rep. Dick Wigley had held for fourteen years. I laughed at them. "What? are you nuts? I've never even been to a Republican caucus?" But they knew that I had lobbied at the national and state level for the restaurant industry, which was true, and had gained valuable experience doing it. A week later two businessmen appeared at my door, Fred Lutz Jr. and Dick Voelz. Not realizing the Republican Party had already asked me, they wanted me to run and suggested that the business community would back me. They said, rather persuasively, that business owners needed a strong voice in the state legislature. As they were leaving, Fred asked if there were a chance I would consider it. "A ten percent chance at best," I said. That night Rose did her best not to laugh too hard at the idea of me as a politician.

I had to learn more. I didn't know what a state legislator did, so I invited Rep. Wigley and his wife, Fran, over for evening coffee, where Rose asked the tough questions while I asked about a legislator's duties, benefits and pay. I didn't want government service to run us into the ground financially. Over the next few weeks we chatted with Sen. Glen Taylor, Glenda Taylor, and Rep. Mark Piepho. Through these discussions we decided all obstacles in our path could be overcome — and we had a sufficient store of personal finances and the business community's backing.

But we hadn't gauged how it would affect Happy Chef. Immediately after I declared for office, the organizer of a 200-person banquet cancelled and a week later the organizer of a 150-person banquet cancelled. Both were from MSU. I learned later that both organizers had taken offense at my status as a Republican candidate. I don't know why, but for some reason these individuals must have held the belief that Republicans hated education and if unchecked would suspend student loans and cut teacher pay and benefits. I wasn't mean-spirited and didn't understand why they, apparently, and others, believed these lies that played on people's fears. Evidently, a lie said loud enough and often enough will be believed by at least a few anxious hearts.

My brothers and I were stunned both personally and professionally by the cancellations. From then on it became rather evident that our business relationship would have to change. I would have to sell out to my brothers.

The business was running along smoothly. To continue on without me all it needed was a capable general manager. Tom decided that Glen Thompson, a banker, was the one man interviewed who could hold together a chain of restaurants scattered all over the Upper Midwest — and he did, being a sound manager, focused on service and talented at handling employees and customers.

People have told me that my main strengths are common sense and organization. If a businessperson isn't organized I have trouble trusting them, even if they are friendly and treated me well. Glen was organized, which meant with him we wouldn't be opening a gaping hole in the organization. I cushioned the blow further by remaining on as a non-paid consultant. (My "pay" over the years has been the respect I receive from my brothers and from Happy Chef employees.)

Our accountants and attorneys had worked out a buy/sell agreement years before so that when I did sell we could use the percentages from the agreement. Bob then decided to sell out with me, and together we stretched the buy-out over ten years so we wouldn't have to burden our two remaining brothers with debt that could muffle expansion plans. I'm very proud of my brothers and what they have accomplished since. The restaurant business was a challenge then, but with the added labor shortage, as with all restaurant chains today, they have had to fight extra hard for success.

After feeling my way through discussions with the Wigleys, Taylors and Mark Piepho, the banquet cancellations, and the sell-out, an overwhelming sense of pressure towards running for state representative began overtaking me. I was, truly, in over my head. In early June 1984, the day after I declared, a woman telephoned to say she wanted to meet with me the next morning at 8:00 a.m. She said she was very pro-life. After hanging up, I telephoned people I trusted within the party. One of them told me to not attend the meeting alone. And the result? Ten people showed for the meeting: on one side were three women, all very pro-life, including the one who had called; and on the other, Rose, myself, and five Republicans to support me. Right away they said, "We want to question you." "About what?" "About being pro-life." "Pro-life?" "We don't think you're pro-life enough and we're going to run someone against you for the nomination."

I waved my hands. "Wait one minute," I said. "My father had eleven brothers and sisters, then he married and had nine children. My Uncle Cletus and his wife, Valeria, had seventeen children. I had eight brothers and sisters. Rose and I have six daughters and ten grandchildren. How much more pro-life do you want?" They were taken aback. I continued on. "But I'll tell you one thing, if I get elected, I will not wear the pro-life issue on my sleeve. I am pro-life and I will be pro-life. But I won't make it my only issue." My speech saddened them and as they sulked away I wondered if they would present a challenge at the nominating convention. Eventually they did float a trial balloon, one that hinted at challenging me, but the balloon must have burst along the way. Raised as a Catholic, I never knew that abortion existed mainly because it wasn't even discussed at home. Our parents taught us to regulate our lives. If we fathered a child out of wedlock the only option would be to marry and raise that child. Abortion was never an option.

My friends knew I would be attacked, but didn't think it would take place so quickly. A few days after the pro-life meeting, the *Free Press* ran a letter to the editor from a woman claiming I had made my money off the backs of my employees, had worked them to death, and been a terrible boss. (I still have the letter.) At the time I thought, What have I gotten myself into? I telephoned the *Free Press* and asked them why they had printed it. They knew me better than that. They reminded me that it was now open season because I had chosen to become a public figure. The *Free Press* could print anything, truth or lie, from any citizen, on its letters to the editor page. I learned that the woman writing the lies was also chairwoman of the Nicollet County DFL Party. After much thought, I mailed off a reply to the *Free Press*. In it I congratulated her for fulfilling her role as a DFL chairwoman and explained to the readers that she had to tear me down because it was her job. From that day forward I never read another word about being a "terrible boss."

To win I needed a good campaign manager to overcome my political naiveté. Glen Taylor suggested Darlene Radichel, whom I tried to persuade, but she refused, saying she had retired after Glen's campaign. A few weeks later Rose and I were at my parent's home in Madison Lake, discussing the need for a campaign manager, when Dad spoke up. "We know Darlene," he said. "She lives by the lake. Why not drop on over?" Even though she had been so adamant in her previous refusal, I was now desperate.

She resisted all my arguments. So I asked, "How about just getting me started?" When she agreed to that, I began peppering her with all my questions: "What do I need? What committees need forming? What types of people need to be on those committees? Could I just meet with you once?" We met later at Happy Chef where she opened her files from Glen's campaign. After the meeting — it must have been the look of hopelessness in my eyes that persuaded her — she agreed to be a "temporary" consultant until I could find a permanent campaign manager. Darlene and I were scouting for one when, at a meeting for Republicans at Happy Chef North, a friend introduced me to Ken Krause. We bonded. I learned of his background, admired his style, and felt I understood him. After the meeting I asked him to be my campaign manager. (He agreed and later managed all my political campaigns.)

An MSU professor, Georgia Holmes, was my opponent in 1984. The Democrat-Farmer-Labor Party in Mankato almost always ran an individual closely tied to education because they felt if they did they could count on the educational community's support — and in Mankato that community was massive, which, when combined with the liberal daily newspaper's support, always turned a Republican's task into an uphill battle from the start.

During the campaign the Minnesota Education Association put me through the ringer and hung me out to dry. Following an interview with them I felt confident that I would receive their support. Boy, was I naive. Apparently they had an agenda and Sal Frederick, an evil Republican, would never be a part of it. A friend of mine, also a teacher, told me that he had, along with others on the local MEA endorsement selection committee, strongly urged the state organization to endorse me. A few weeks later he showed me the state MEA's response, which thanked the selection committee for their effort but explained that they didn't endorse Republicans. My friend argued with them but he could have been arguing with a curtain rod. (Since then, the MEA, now Educate Minnesota, has endorsed a few Republicans but only those in "safe" seats.)

The campaign began catching fire. I very much wanted to carry my hometown, Madison Lake, a DFL stronghold, and to do it I thought I needed to visit with Madison Lake resident Doc Shepard, who was a top DFL fundraiser. It did pay dividends because he pledged to not work against me, which was the next best thing to an endorsement. Dick Wigley had earlier advised me to forget Madison Lake.

The idea of having to debate an MSU professor trained to deliver effective presentations really began rattling me. I had not taken speech in high school. In any Mankato debate two-thirds of the audience was made up of Democrats. There weren't enough business owners in Mankato with the free time to attend a debate and the rest wouldn't because their DFL customers had threatened to stop doing business with them. It happened more than once: a DFL'er would telephone a business owner and tell them to not back me in public or else they would risk losing them as customers. A few of my supporters knuckled under. One supporter, Willie Negaard, a restaurant owner who later ran for state senate, told them to "stick it where the sun don't shine."

A former Happy Chef employee who owned a North Mankato catering business courageously planted a "Frederick" sign outside her building. It was a courageous act because she was also the caterer for the Teamster's annual picnic until a Teamster demanded that she "take down that sign or we won't have our picnic with you." "I'm sorry, but I'm not going to do it," she said, unwaveringly, "because Sal taught me everything I know, and I wouldn't be here if it wasn't for him." They took the business from her but gave it back the next year. They weren't very happy with her replacement.

CHAPTER EIGHT

Minnesotans should respect all their elected officials for the many sacrifices they make of their time, energy, and money, and for their effort in choosing to take on the very puzzling process called the state legislature — at least Rose and I thought everyone should do that soon after I was sworn in!

As a rookie state representative, I went to bat for a Madison Lake man in what evolved into the classic example of government bureaucracy run amuck. Jon Schneider had built a gazebo on his lakefront property in Madison Lake and in doing so had cleared it of assorted junk, ragweed and poison ivy. This new gazebo landscaped with railroad ties was so impressive that boaters floated over just to indulge in its beauty. The Minnesota Department of Natural Resources promptly informed Jon that he had violated a law by building his gazebo — this, despite its having passed City of Madison Lake muster. It was only then that the City of Madison Lake and Jon learned for the first time that the DNR legally controlled one thousand feet out from the lakeshore, which meant half the city of Madison Lake had been under DNR control for years without their knowledge. The DNR ordered Jon to restore his property to its primitive state of ragweed and poison ivy. At that juncture Jon and I began spinning around the Ferris wheel of bureaucratic madness while the DNR held the stop and go levers. Eventually they let him keep his gazebo but with restrictions.

When average citizens negotiated with a state agency, often they ran up against large egos that seemed as if they had to "win" just to impress their many bosses. Many a state agency decision lacked rhyme or reason — strangling a particular situation until all rational thought and common sense was ignored. There were exceptions to the rule. For example, the City of St. Clair had been trying to bring in Goodrich Acres, a new development, when negotiations faltered and St. Clair resident Floyd Palmer asked me for assistance in keeping it on track. I was able to persuade Peter Gillette, the commissioner of the Department of Trade and Economic Development (DTED), to visit the proposed site. He was very impressed with what the residents were doing for themselves. The people of St. Clair later told me that he was the highest-ranking state official ever to visit their town. The visit worked, DTED assisted, and the subdivision helped grow St. Clair.

At the State Capitol I began wondering when all the MEA teachers found the time to teach the children they said they loved so much when almost every day one faction or another of them was there lobbying the legislature — and being paid to do it with taxpayer dollars. If they had lobbied to produce a better student I would have welcomed them with open arms. In early 1992 an MEA delegation visited my office on a morning when I was away in committee. To suit their request for a meeting, my secretary, Kathy Anderson, told them my room number after which they marched down the hall and persuaded a page to interrupt the committee proceedings. They wanted to talk with me. I told the page that I couldn't leave then because the committee was nearing a vote. Later I did go out to see them during a recess. One of them, who said they were seeking better teacher benefits, said they wanted to talk with me right then in my office.

"The only way I'll meet with you," I said as years of frustration began tumbling freely off my lips, "is if you have a plan to turn a better product out of our schools. I get so much heat from people who hire high school graduates that can't read, write and do simple math." I shifted my weight from one foot to the other and began pointing my index finger at them. "Not only that," I continued on, "but students entering technical college have to take remedial programs to get up to speed. Unless you have a plan, I won't talk to you." The teachers hemmed and hawed and after I turned away to finish the committee agenda I heard one of them say, "I told you Frederick would be a hard nut to crack." It seemed as if all the teachers union ever really cared about was its own member's financial success. They vehemently resisted any plan that rewarded or penalized teachers according to individual performance.

In the late '80s the MEA pushed a bill through that fined a school district twenty-five dollars a day per student if any school district hadn't settled its contract with the teachers union prior to January 15 of that year. In other words, the taxpayers would be fined when a school board and the union couldn't settle, but the union wasn't fined if they held out. Outrageous bills like this soured me on them and on politics in general. Whenever I brought asinine bills like this to the *Free Press's* attention its reporters shrugged their shoulders. If you were in the majority, they said, you wouldn't be so upset. But they were dead wrong. If the Republicans were in the majority and passing similar bills, I would have raised a major stink.

One truth about politics I learned the hard way: anyone being overly friendly to me was doing it for a reason, almost always in an attempt to use me for their own personal or organizational gain. I avoided these bloodsuckers like I would the Plague.

The competitive nature of St. Paul politics disturbed me. My brothers and I had built Happy Chef on a foundation of teamwork in a family atmosphere. In the legislature there were politicians who tried to shake everything up by insisting that their ideas were the only ones that ought to be considered. The best legislators, in my opinion, respected "team" members from both parties, meandered around problems, and worked towards consensus. Not everyone liked a final solution arrived at this way but all should have been able to live with it before moving on to the next agenda item.

St. Paul had 201 legislators and some of them never forgave or forgot. If a Republican strongly opposed a Democrat, he was put on a "hit" list, which meant they would try to push him around. Apparently I must have opposed a Democrat once or twice because I was informed one day that I would be fined fifty dollars a day for failing to turn in my financial report as required by law — a revelation that, if leaked to a press hungry for dirt on Republicans, would have been a public relations nightmare. But I need not have worried. Robert Kitchenmaster, a CPA and my campaign treasurer, had sent my financial report to the state board in time and he had a returned certified mail receipt to prove it. When he heard about the threatened fine, he drove to the Ethical Practices Board to show them the proof. They couldn't argue with that. Two years later, the board tried pulling the same stunt again. Thanks Bob for a job well done.

I wouldn't trade my eight years at the legislature in for anything. It was another learning experience on the menu of my life. I faced constant adversity and yet was able to accomplish good for the people of Minnesota and for my district. I'm proud of starting the drug prevention program in Region Nine. At times young people need a push in the right direction. I'm proud of establishing a Port Authority in North Mankato, a bill that allowed that city to expand faster. While I was explaining the Port Authority bill on the House floor, several DFL'ers tried ridiculing it. "What lake is that in Mankato? Do you really need a Port Authority? Is it a pond you have in Mankato?" They really let me have it, but ultimately they had to admit that North Mankato had been a focal point for river commerce into the early 1900s.

Being a minority party member was much easier than being in the majority because we couldn't initiate any reform bills — and therefore didn't have to work as hard. I didn't enjoy that. The majority had all the responsibility. I desired reform often opposite to the "reform" proposed by the DFL majority. I read recently where a minority DFL state representative from Mankato said really all he could do in the legislature was lob bombs at the majority. He was bored. When I was in the legislature, a minority member could try to pass a bill, but doing it was like spitting into the wind. If it was a good idea the DFL would let you do all the legwork for them, then one of their members would steal all your hard work and introduce a similar bill. The Republican bill would never receive a hearing.

In the late '80s, at a Mankato Chamber function with Sen. Glen Taylor and Rep. John Dorn, I looked out at the audience and noticed the usual hands popping up to ask the questions. The first questioner asked for our stands on the minimum wage, to which Glen and I offered clear and concise answers while Rep. Dorn droned on for five minutes to eat up time so he wouldn't have to answer as many questions. He always seemed slightly uncomfortable at chamber of commerce functions. At the end of Rep. Dorn's speech and before the moderator could prompt another questioner, I raised my hand. "Wait a minute," I said as all eyes swung towards me. "He didn't answer the question." The moderator turned to the questioner, who said, "Sal is right. He didn't answer it." He repeated his question and this time Rep. Dorn spoke so softly I couldn't even hear him — and I was on the dais with him. The moderator, apparently satisfied with Rep. Dorn's answer, began pointing at hands again. That did it. "Wait one minute!" I said, waving a hand. "I'm sitting right here and I couldn't hear him." I turned towards Rep. Dorn. "Will you, John, vote for or against a raise in minimum wage?" Even then only the people in front heard him. Political forums frustrated me because audiences seldom demanded a yes or no answer from a candidate. Often the audience walked away knowing even less about a candidate's position than before the function started.

I was the restaurant industry's banner carrier and as such stoked a few House floor fires over important industry issues. One year a special interest group tried to ban all cheese processed outside Minnesota from being sold in Minnesota. It was an asinine bill because Roquefort and many other cheeses weren't being processed by anyone in Minnesota. In the fight I gained a DFL ally, Rep. Phyllis Kahn, who recognized its idiocy. Rep. Andy Steensma, a DFL farmer from western Minnesota, began attacking my ally and me and Steensma was losing when DFL Rep. Trimble tried rescuing him, which worsened matters for both because neither knew anything about the industry. While at a lobbyist's party after the floor debate, Rep. Steensma's wife snubbed Rose because I had made her husband lose the debate.

In 1986 I led the charge on allowing outstate restaurants to compete with their metro counterparts when selling liquor. Before my bill outstate restaurants couldn't serve liquor until noon on Sunday while metro restaurants could begin at 10:00 a.m. Happy Chef didn't sell liquor, but the restaurant owners who did were saying it wasn't fair that bars in the seven-county metro area could serve earlier. Their complaints moved me to author a bill that would set liquor serving times back two hours for the entire state. It seemed every anti-liquor person in Minnesota called my office to complain. In defense of the bill, I argued on the House floor that restaurant owners should be permitted to sell hard drinks earlier because those drinks, in essence, were food products. Alcohol was manufactured from grain. The Star Tribune quoted me on that, everyone laughed, but not one person proved me wrong. Minnesota restaurants can now serve liquor at 10:00 a.m. on Sunday.

Out-of-control government growth and spending frustrated me because it hamstrung the ability of businesses — and therefore everyone in the state, including the poor — to reach their maximum potential for prosperity. I felt state government had tried taking over the role of being our neighbor. Years ago when a person went through shaky times it was the community which helped them, not the government. In those more neighborly days everybody cared for each other. In modern society people don't have to know their neighbor's names because when they do need help they have the government to turn to instead.

Do you know how state government raises taxes without you even knowing it? I do. I watched the tax and spenders at work in the state legislature. They raised your taxes when they added a tax to a segment of the business community. The business owners objected to this, of course, but there were only a few of them. After the business added the new tax into the price of the product you bought, you complained to them about higher prices. The business then had to collect and send the tax on to the government. The business took the heat, the government used the business as a tax collector, and once again your pocket was picked by a tax and spend legislator.

Without Rose's aid and comfort the pressures of politics would have overwhelmed me. Her personality helped legislators and lobbyists feel comfortable, and she broke the ice in hundreds of conversations with her laughter, wit and warm conversation. Some spouses didn't help their husbands or wives, which compounded the stress of being at the state legislature.

Legislators from both sides and their spouses seemed to like us because we tried to not be too critical of anyone and, for the most part, tolerated opposing viewpoints. When we disagreed with another legislator it was done with tact. Rose and I bent over backwards to get along with Democrats because it was in our nature to do that. I never allowed myself to get sucked into an argument with anyone who rigidly espoused an opposing viewpoint, for the reason that I couldn't change them or their views and it would only lead to hard feelings.

In 1984 we couldn't have elected a better Speaker of the House than Dave Jennings. He was intelligent, quick-minded, frugal, a sensible manager, and he didn't tolerate political posturing. The lowest point of my eight years in office was the day Dave resigned as Speaker — it devastated me, as if I had lost my best friend. He was burned out and both the liberal press and DFL were constantly sniping at him. The Democrats had been in power twenty-five years and many weren't coping well with being out of it — much like a heroin addict feels without a fix. In fact, if they had lost the House again in 1986, many of their legislators would have retired rather than continue in the minority. Several of them personally told me that.

After 1986 I had to represent the Mankato area alongside Rep. John Dorn, a likeable, party-line Democrat, and an educator, which translated into being a union man who voted yes on nearly every anti-business bill — even though he often said the opposite at town meetings. The average voter seldom followed his votes. Most believed what he said at town meetings, chamber events and forums. I couldn't tell you how many times I heard, "But he said he supports business!" To which I always replied, "He says it, but look at his votes." John Dorn wasn't the only DFL'er to do this.

Many news reporters wrote from a liberal bias, which puzzled me then and now because newspapers, as for-profit businesses, are regularly damaged by anti-business DFL policy. One explanation for the bias could be because Minnesota has been so liberal for so long the reporters write to fit the "perceived" audience. The only newspaper in the entire state to back Congressman Gil Gutknecht (R-Rochester) in 1994 was the Maple River Messenger, a 1,700-circulation weekly. Imagine: Gil won his congressional district with fifty-seven percent of the vote and with the endorsement of less than one percent of the state's newspapers — just one example of the bias against Republicans.

While I was in the legislature, I mailed several press releases to the *Free Press* to inform its readers on timely and significant issues and the *Free Press* never printed them. In one instance a *Free Press* employee telephoned an organization in Massachusetts to check on the accuracy of one of my releases. In it I had referred to Massachusetts as "Taxachusetts" and backed my claim with statistics from this organization. Compare this to their response to the Democrat who slid a letter under their door — with inaccuracies, half-truths and false accusations — and without verification they printed it in the next day's paper. Too much proof of their bias existed to say it was just my perception.

I'm convinced that if the mainstream media wasn't so mean-spirited towards conservatives, Republicans in Minnesota would have a much bigger and therefore better pool of candidates from which to choose for public office. With a fairer media the people of Minnesota would be the winners because they would have the best candidates. In the past, many conservatives haven't run for office because they feared what the media would do to them.

Some politicians said and did anything to remain in power. Take Sen. Roger Moe, for example, who ran his campaigns from inside the State Capitol. Three years after the Republicans removed its reelection committees outside the Capitol in order to separate those duties from legislative business, as they properly should have, Roger Moe was still mixing the two, which meant, whether willingly or unwillingly, that every taxpayer across the state was helping to reelect him and his fellow DFL members. A member of his staff finally blew the whistle.

As the dominant party in 1990, the DFL was charged with redistricting, which was the duty of redrawing legislative districts according to the population ebb and flow since the previous census. It is done every ten years. To determine how it could best benefit them, the DFL set up shop in two offices at the state office building directly across the hall from mine and worked twenty-four-hour days. At 3:00 a.m. (yes, I put in long hours) I once watched DFL'ers with tired eyes dart in and out of the redistricting planning rooms. No one could enter the redistricting room without direct permission from the Democrats.

Their redistricting plan placed my home in Mankato Township at the southernmost tip of a new district that stretched north over twenty miles to Le Sueur. I had been close to the center of my old district but now only three pieces of it remained: North Mankato, Lyme Township and Mankato Township. It just so happened that the rest of the new district had been part of Rep. Don Ostrom's old district. In essence, the DFL redistricting group placed me in Ostrom's district where he was entrenched and forced me to run against him to keep my seat. Ostrom and I were the only incumbents in the entire state who had to run against each other. Obviously, the DFL wanted me out. By then, Rep. Dorn had ousted Mark Piepho, and Rep. Ostrom had beaten Al Quist. I must have been a sore spot to them as the only Republican in the area.

Republican Gov. Arne Carlson could have vetoed the redistricting plan but the Democrats tricked him into not doing it. Here was how they did it: When Rudy Perpich was governor, bills passed at the end of session were slid under his door before midnight and the next day he would "technically" sign or veto and then date them as the day before. No one raised an eyebrow at his practice. When the DFL presented their redistricting plan to Gov. Carlson, they slid the bill under his door the same way as before. Arne vetoed the bill the next day and backdated it. The DFL then claimed the veto wasn't binding because it was signed after midnight — and technically they were correct. Their actions reinforced what I already knew, that politics was a dirty game.

Politics In Minnesota, a magazine devoted to state politics and popular among political junkies and state legislators, predicted that I would lose to Rep. Ostrom by 2,000 votes because two-thirds of the voters in the new district were from his old district. The actual vote count would be a lot closer. Election night at VFW Post 950 in Mankato was an emotional roller coaster — up one minute, down another, roaring through the dark tunnel of doubt and climbing steeply towards elation — as the vote count flip-flopped all evening. I was leading with only one St. Peter precinct, Gustavus Adolphus College, yet to report, but that one went to Ostrom, who appeared to have won by 42 votes. Later, after a recount, I gained three votes to lose by 39.

Once the recount was final I telephoned Rep. Ostrom and congratulated him for his election victory. I had put out 110 percent and couldn't have done anything extra to win. The sour taste of losing such a close election didn't stay in my mouth long. I believe my hardworking committee members took the loss harder than I did.

After losing in 1992, people still asked for my help and advice, sometimes over a cup of coffee or on the telephone — and it's still happening today. A total stranger telephoned me in December 1999 and over a twenty-five minute period she sought my advice and help on an idea her husband had of buying a 200-acre farm. I gave her advice but couldn't give her the full help she requested because I wasn't a legislator anymore. I did give her names to call.

At my funeral I hope people remember me as a man who loved his family, used his time wisely, was honest, decent, down-to-earth, and cared about others. I have tried to continually help business owners by being an ambassador for the Mankato Area Chamber & Convention Bureau. I am now serving as president, in 1999-2000, of the newly formed Mankato Rehabilitation Center Foundation, which supports people with disabilities and disadvantages so they can achieve a more meaningful participation in society. (In 1971, Happy Chef received the Minnesota State Award for being pioneers in hiring the developmentally disabled.) The Foundation will have to make something beautiful out of nothing because we're starting it from scratch. Another exciting and rewarding endeavor in 1999 was being co-president with Rose of the revitalized Katoland Connection (the former 30-40 Club). This reunion group unites people who have or had an interest in Mankato and its surrounding area.

* * *

In 1998 I helped Julie Storm (R-St.Peter) win her

legislative seat. Politicians are only as good as their word and Julie has kept hers. I believe you can't truly know a person until you have worked with them on a committee where you can observe their work ethic. I have worked on committees with Julie and have seen her enthusiasm rub off on colleagues. Julie Storm loves her work and gives it her all. In many ways, I see a bit of myself in her.

    And then there was Rep. Tim Penny. Congressman Penny talked conservative out on the farms and with businessmen, but the talk didn't match the walk. An example was his 1993 vote for the largest tax bill in U.S. history. The Democrat power structure needed only one vote for its passage and it was his. His vote upset me because I had personally telephoned his office and was told by his aide that Penny would never vote for the bill because it was "bad for southern Minnesota." About two hundred people called his office that day and received the same pat answer. Betraying his constituency for what his Washington bosses commanded him to do must have ate at his conscience because he declared soon thereafter that he wouldn't be seeking another term. After Congress he became highly critical of politics inside the Washington Beltway. I personally felt betrayed by his vote. I was meeting with a group of bankers from Mankato in 1998 when several of them learned for the first time, from me, that Penny had actually voted for the tax increase. Like me, they had called and been told he would never vote for it. But once again, like so many people, they never bothered to check his vote.

CHAPTER NINE

In 1982 I met Martin Tonn when he was seeking private venture capital for a brilliant invention that would provide farmers an alternative to gasoline, which had been in short supply at times in the '70s. The federal government was offering tax credits then to encourage research of alternative energy sources — and eventually it was these legal tax credits the IRS used to go after me. They claimed I had invested in Martin's invention solely for the credits and not with the intent to establish a real business and hire employees. They were dead wrong, wrong to this day, and always will be wrong. A CPA testified in court that he had figured my tax return correctly. Again, I believe the IRS was picking on a smaller company that didn't have the resources to fight them in order to use us as an example to the whole alternative fuel industry. We didn't appreciate their heavy-handed, brown shirt tactics then, and I don't to this day. Out of Martin's thirty-nine investors, only five took the tax credit; the rest were farmers seeking a low-cost means to plant, cultivate and harvest crops. Martin's invention made so much sense it couldn't fail. And it would have been a success — and revolutionized farm life for tens of thousands of rural families — had the IRS not declared the business a tax scheme and shut it down.

If Martin Tonn's invention had been allowed to blossom, many farmers wouldn't have had to sell their equipment and leave the industry. With the invention, a farmer could produce ethanol and other valuable by-products on his own farm, using his own corn. A farmer shelled his corn off the cob, tossed the cob into a gasifier, fermented the starch into a sugar and made ethanol from it. A high-protein mash from the process increased a dairy herd's milk production. CO_2 from the process could be piped into greenhouses. Farmers could sell homegrown vegetables to grocery stores during the lengthy Minnesota winters. Not an ounce of product was wasted. An engine running on ethanol leaves no pollution whatsoever, only a sweet smelling vapor from the exhaust.

Martin Tonn bought a technologically advanced facility in Wisconsin, and ultimately he employed sixty-five people.

Ethanol, Martin discovered, could be produced from most any grain. Sweet sorghum seemed the best suited because it didn't require cooking; it was already a sugar and cheaper per gallon to manufacture. The business worked in conjunction with Mankato Technical Institute, had several demonstration plots near Good Thunder, Minn., and it rented a combine harvester. The plant also manufactured forage boxes designed to collect the chopped corn or hay. As a sideline, it was close to reaching an agreement with the U.S. Government to manufacture brakes for new military vehicles, and it had consummated a deal to do all of John Deere's lawn mower and garden equipment painting for them in Wisconsin. The plant had the only EPA-approved and certified paint booth in the state. We even manufactured some John Deere lawn mowers.

Some of the investors cut off their support after the IRS claimed Martin had taken the money and wasn't investing it into the plant. When the money stopped flowing in, the plant controller held back on paying the necessary FICA taxes in order to satisfy the claims of several vendors. The Internal Revenue Service seized the plant for non-payment of FICA taxes and sent the workers home — not even letting them take their lunch buckets with them. To remedy the situation, we hand carried $30,000, as a good faith payment to the bank to assure that the IRS would let the company continue operating. The payment was not put in the intended trust fund, but in the company's tax account by mistake. The IRS claimed in its initial case against us that our company had never been a business even though they had sent sixty-five of our employees home the day of the seizure. Talking to them was like screaming into a vacuum. It took Martin two months to learn why they had closed the plant.

Several people suggested that my IRS troubles were related to my politics — and were just another dirty trick aimed at a Republican. I discounted that theory. But I have had suspicions that an oil company or companies were behind the negative press about ethanol. As vice-chair of the House Commerce Committee I held hearings to investigate assertions that oil companies were deliberately sabotaging ethanol's name. (The hearings were justified given the recent growth in ethanol plant construction and the demand for ethanol from the state's corn growers.) In the hearings, several oil company executives locked onto my eyes, claimed innocence, and denied any involvement whatsoever.

My life began on a modest Madison Lake farm and because of that my heart always has been with the average Minnesota farmer. Martin's invention could have helped many ordinary farmers make it through extraordinary times. I saw his invention working, touched it with my hands and smelled its sweet exhaust fumes. Perhaps Martin Tonn was ahead of his time. In the spring of 2000 one of his units was still running at a farm near St.Cloud, Minn.

Martin, who is burdened by owing so much to his investors, has dedicated his remaining years to paying them back. Despite coercion from the IRS, not one investor has deserted him since the plant closing. He could sell his technology but won't because he wants to make right the IRS wrong. It's amazing to think that the cause of such heartache for one decent man, his investors, and for thousands of family farms all over America who would have benefited from the invention was an IRS that shot first before asking questions. I don't see how some of their agents can sleep at night.

Bird's eye view of Indian Lake Ranch

CHAPTER TEN

Dr. Mickelson built Indian Lake Ranch in 1949 on the most scenic hilltop in the Mankato area, and furnished it with about 5,000 sq. ft. of floor space, including a full basement, six bedrooms and three baths. He registered the 40 acres of property with the state of Minnesota as a tree farm. When Rose heard it was for sale, she talked me into driving over to see it for myself. It was early evening and a gentle breeze was blowing in from the west, softened by the thousands of leafy trees that covered the hilltop and valley. A striking view of Mount Kato, a skiing mecca for all southern Minnesota, was set out before our eyes. "It will be great for the girls," Rose said as she inhaled the fresh hilltop air through smiling lips. To which I replied, "It's a big house, but I'm sold on the property."

The owner, Jim Maslon, Indian Lake Ranch's second owner and a Honeymead vice-president, was generous with terms. We bought three acres around the home and left the rest to him. It seemed a great deal at the time. Later, while signing papers at the attorney's office for the closing, we verbally agreed that I would have first right of refusal on the remaining thirty-seven acres. His attorney thought that was a bad idea and tried to talk him out of putting it into writing. Jim at least verbally agreed to it and, in the presence of the attorney, awarded me first right of refusal with a firm handshake.

Years later he wanted to sell the land. His real estate agent told me what he had to have for the property and I swallowed hard. He was asking a California price for rural Minnesota land. I refused his offer. Six years later, with the thirty-seven acres still on the open market and not one serious buyer in his sights, Jim softened his stance significantly to where I could sign a ten-year contract for deed. Despite the six-year disagreement over price, our relationship was so friendly that after the contract was fulfilled I still made a few payments. (At tax time I realized I had overpaid beyond the ten years and he refunded several checks.)

Soon after we purchased the ranch, my brother-in-law, Jim Keckeisen, brought over a brass, Japanese submarine telescope on the Fourth of July and from ten miles away we watched the parade in St. Peter. On winter evenings I have been able to open my living room drapes and read the newspaper from the glare of Mount Kato's spotlights reflecting off the snow. One time as I was flying towards Mankato from the west in the dead of winter I noticed what seemed like a brilliant fire. "What the devil is that?" I asked the pilot. "That's Mount Kato. We use it as a beacon light for Mankato in the winter."

In the mid-'80s I started a book that contains all my photographs of some of the wildlife on our property: fox, possum, deer, turkeys, raccoons, squirrels. Last year I counted thirty-six turkeys parading across the yard at one time.

We will leave our home one day, but never our home of Mankato whose people have treated us so wonderfully throughout the years. Our children don't want us to sell Indian Lake Ranch because their children, our grandchildren, absolutely adore it. They load vans with friends from the Twin Cities and use the grounds for birthday parties and picnics. A Lutheran church leader asked if she could have a party for their youth on our land, and then it dawned on me that the Catholic youth from our parish had never asked for it. Her request was fine because we get along with everybody. These requests are common now.

Our pool opens early June and closes right after Labor Day. I swim almost every day for the recreation and quiet, and especially so during stretches of hot temperatures and high humidity. I need the break from a busy day. Fifteen minutes of paddling or floating around refreshes the body and cleans the cobwebs from the mind. Overall, I feel very blessed with my life so far...and it isn't over yet!

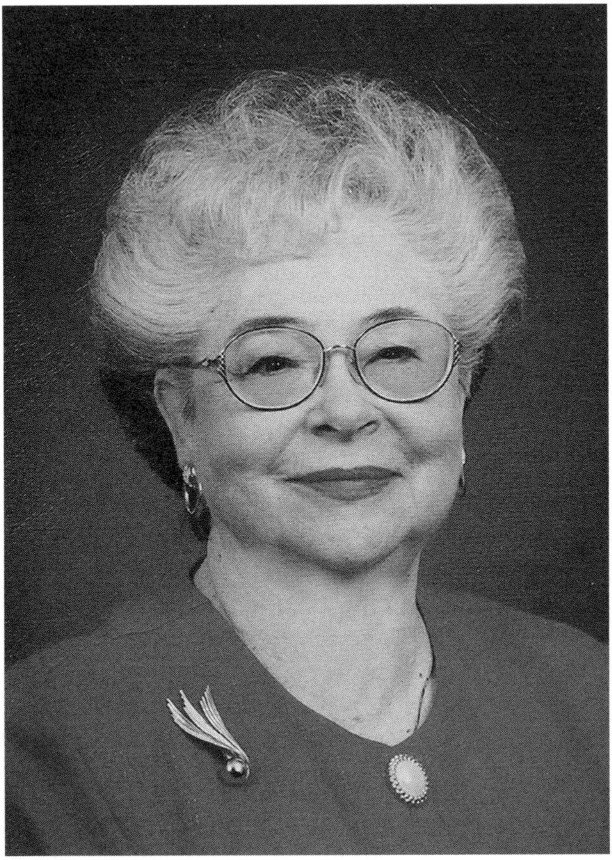

CHAPTER ELEVEN
by ROSE

I have to get the last word in about my Sal.

I met him at the Saulpaugh Hotel. The head chef there, Ray, had hired me to baby-sit his own kids and my compensation for it, besides the pay, was a free meal. My first day eating there a young man walked over, introduced himself as "Sal" and took my food order as he would most nights thereafter. One evening a waitress who had dyed-red hair and a hard-as-nails temperament walked over and asked me if I was having an affair with this Sal. I was taken aback and swallowed hard, primarily because I didn't understand what she meant by an "affair." I was 15 and very innocent. She said I had to be having an affair with him because he let me order food off the menu while the other employees had to eat leftovers. Even though he was five years older, I began thinking of him in a different light from that night on. He impressed me: he was an army veteran, a high school graduate, kind, and a gentleman.

Sal had to overcome adversity just from a nickname, "Sally," that was the taunt of every schoolboy. In the army he witnessed atrocities firsthand and the aftermath of two atomic bombs, was exposed to nuclear radiation, and later was hounded and harassed by the IRS, the Democrats and a liberal media. Yet he never allowed any of it to bother him much, choosing instead to go with the flow more than any other person I knew. He didn't sweat what he couldn't control.

When we finally began dating our only obstacle centered on my young age that made it difficult for me to drink and socialize at bars along with his friends. Usually Sal and his friends didn't invite me along because of it and the few times they did, even though I drank Coke through a straw, it wasn't much fun because I was paranoid of my dad finding out.

In a strange way I was glad that Sal hurt his back in the army and couldn't farm like his father. Imagine me as a farmer's wife. The first time he drove me to his parents' farm I wore white Capri pants and a peasant blouse with pink ruffles. His brother Bill threw a garter snake onto my chest as I was climbing out the car. I jumped back in, rolled up the windows and wouldn't budge until Sal's mother — trying hard not to laugh — somehow talked me out. I saw the Fredericks make blood sausage, which they had every intention of feeding to me at breakfast the next day. Another weekend they were butchering chickens when one of the chickens began running around the barnyard with its head cut off, with blood spurting everywhere, and I'm back safe in the car again.

I married in October 1949 when I was but 17, four months after graduating from Loyola High School. Sal's mother said to him that marrying me might be a big mistake because I was too young and would be "trouble." On the other hand, my mother adored Sal and told me that when I "have marital problems don't come knocking at my door because I know it will be your fault. Work them out yourself." So I went to Grandma who was three blocks away. All the older ladies in the neighborhood thought we married because I was pregnant, but that wasn't the case. Our first daughter wasn't born until 1952.

Our honeymoon in California was spent at the home of my aunt Mildred and her husband. After we left her home for Minnesota, Mildred wrote to a relative: "Loved having Rosemary and Sal here but she's just a little girl playing house. Their marriage is never going to last." I really wanted her at our fiftieth wedding anniversary but at the time she was 91 and in California. I was tempted to call her to say, "nyah, nyah, nyah, nyah, nyah," but didn't because she had lost her hearing by then and her sense of humor. Instead I sent an invitation that read, "Wish you could join us."

Just the mere thought of waitressing scared me because I had never done anything but eat in a restaurant my whole life. I didn't know what I would do when Sal said the only way he could make a go of the Hidden Inn would be for me to be its waitress. I called my friend Evie Fasnacht, who had worked at the Wagon Wheel, and even though she was pregnant she agreed to teach me. She said if I didn't catch on by the end of two weeks I never would, which made me all the more nervous. When she left two weeks later I had thirteen stools and two booths and to keep orders straight I glued numbers to my side of the counter so I would know which order went with which person. I worked from 7:00 a.m. to a break in the afternoon in a closet of a restaurant that had smokers for customers and a dreadful air exchange system. When I trudged the aisle of the city bus towards home every afternoon the regular bus riders smelled me coming a mile away. I was "the fried onions and smoke lady."

As a people person too, I eventually fought through my nervousness at work to where I actually began enjoying it and, more importantly, enjoying the regular customers. We developed a relationship with two men in particular who asked for toast and tea every morning. One day after I went home early owing to a burned hand the pair drove over to my house and asked me to make toast and tea for them. We were family to them. I told them to make the toast and tea themselves and they did. Sal, who thought their charade was very funny, really heard an earful from me.

While pregnant with my first child and reaching up for a pack of cigarettes on the top shelf, a few of the women from Automatic Electric having lunch at the Hidden Inn said I could be wrapping my baby's cord around its neck — an unwelcome thought to a pregnant woman. Their warnings frightened me so much I began asking customers to get their own cigarettes.

When Sal tells people that I raised our children he is underreporting his efforts because I couldn't have raised them all alone. When we owned the Corner Cafe Sal and I alternated caring for the kids. And later, even though he was always busy with Happy Chef, he still came home most nights. Most days he would leave home at 5:00 a.m. and return late in the evening. If he dropped by home at all in the day it would be for a few hours in the afternoon. Through it all I was able to realize that his long workdays would end one day. I helped out by making everything run smoothly at home.

My sister-in-law, Anne, forfeited much when she and her husband, Bob, decided to move from South St. Paul, where he had a good job at Swift, to Mankato and help at the Corner Cafe. And yet Bob had never fit into St. Paul, where his small town work ethic kept him at odds with coworkers. Other Swift employees told him he was making them all look bad. Bob shrugged off their complaints, even when they threatened him in the parking lot. Still, Anne did choose to leave a nice new home and follow Bob to a dreary basement apartment on Mound Avenue in Mankato. I have always admired her for that because she took a great risk in choosing to move. Happy Chef wouldn't have happened without them.

Many feminists today seem to believe that marriage should be a fifty-fifty proposition or even that they should have more career opportunities than their man. I was a free spirit, then as now, but realized that in the long run what Sal was doing would be best for both of us, so I seldom resisted any of his business decisions.

Of course, back then most women raised their children at home. Maybe I'm old-fashioned but I have never fully understood the reasoning of women who give birth to a child then two weeks later hire someone else to raise them. Why have a child if you are not going to raise them? When Sal and I were taking turns caring for the kids while we owned the Corner Cafe, and it was my turn at work, I can't tell you how many times I yearned to be home caring for them.

Work wasn't always fun. At the Corner Cafe a drunk stumbled in from driving his car and asked me what day, month, and year it was, and the name of the town. I said, "Mankato." When he received his hot beef commercial, he passed out and his face slumped into his hot food. To keep him from drowning, I gently lifted his head smeared with gravy and mashed potatoes. Bob laughed so hard tears streamed down his cheeks. I wiped the customer's face with a bar towel while Bob called the police. Before the police arrived the customer awoke and handed me his entire key ring chock full of keys because I "was such a nice lady." I still have them.

One of our regular customers, Glen, a shell-shocked veteran from WWII, always wore a white tuxedo jacket year around and carried various items with him: a railroad switchman's lantern, a pint of rubbing alcohol, a thermos bottle. One night Glen strolled in with a fishing rod and reel. He asked for his customary hot coffee. As I was walking away I heard the "whirr" of his fishing line being cast out and then felt a hook catch the back of my uniform. I had to back peddle towards him to keep him from tearing my uniform. Once again Bob was brought to tears from gazing at yet another strange spectacle.

During one stretch in the '50s I gave birth to two children in an eleven-month span, which meant two in diapers and later two in the "terrible twos" at one time. Driven to the point of insanity in caring for them, I remember talking with Grandma while cradling one child in my right arm, the other hand was stirring dinner on the stove, the child not being held was bawling her head off and I was yelling at the others to be quiet. "Grandma, I don't think I'm ever going to get over this," I said between heaving sobs. She reassured me that it would all pass one day and it did.

Our family, 1966 (L to R: Mary, Becky, Peggy, Kathi, Rose, Vicky, Molly, Sal)

After they matured somewhat, Sal and I began disciplining them as a team. The kids were smart and tried pitting one of us against the other, but their cute tactics hardly ever worked. One nightfall with all eight of us at the kitchen table, the kids, in unison, asked for a cottage by the lake because one of their friends had one and being there had been so much fun for them. Sal countered with a suggestion for a swimming pool — it was cheaper and less work, he said — but they kept peppering him with their "cottage by the lake." That night in bed Sal and I heard them whispering to each other and they thought they had talked us into it. Little did they realize that Sal and I were dead set against it. The next morning they put Molly, the youngest, forward. "Dad, can we get a cottage out at the lake?" she asked. Sal said "no."

The kids decided that a family vote should settle the swimming pool or cottage by the lake debate. To humor them, Sal agreed. Six hands shot up for a cottage. Two for a swimming pool. Sal proclaimed "The swimming pool wins!" and the kids nearly rioted. Sal said, "The guy who pays the bills and his wife get four votes each." If only I had tape-recorded their noisy backlash. A swimming pool was built in 1971.

Raising our children became difficult when Sal was named president of the Minnesota Restaurant Association and he regularly had to travel to Minneapolis, which meant I had to be both mother and dad. He always was in such a rush, dashing home, changing clothes, grabbing a sandwich, and then driving off. It became somewhat of a financial burden, especially when Sal was named to the National Restaurant Association board and wasn't reimbursed for his travel to the board meetings. (It was also a financial challenge after we bought Indian Lake Ranch in 1968 and didn't sell the other home in Southview until 1971, which meant Sal had to carry two mortgages, six children, and me, a stay-at-home mom.)

Happy Chef North wasn't open two weeks when a fight erupted outside the restaurant between a stalled motorist and a tow truck driver. The fight spilled into the restaurant, and the two ran through the dining room, tipped over tables and chairs, and stained the new carpet with their blood. In like fashion, soon after Happy Chef East in Mankato opened, a mentally disturbed woman came in and began screaming foul words. Employees were trying to calm her when she picked up a catsup bottle and threw it, denting the wall near the office door. The police arrived and had to toss a net over her.

Sal nearly always called when out of town but the few times he forgot I couldn't sleep for worrying about him, as he traveled through six states on icy roads and through snowy whiteouts.

In the early morning hours once, in the mid-'60s, about

2:00 a.m., the doorbell rang and outside were two strange men. Seeing them frightened me terribly. Sal was away on business. They wanted to use my telephone because their car was stuck on the main road. I offered to call AAA for them but they weren't members. With that I told them to please find another home and telephone. I needed Sal that night.

Mother's Day was invariably a lonely day for me because Sal had to work on what was Happy Chef's highest grossing day of the year. The kids and I attended church and ate without him. That loneliness was part of the price I paid for the life we chose.

We ate dinner one evening with friends. Sal had to leave early to monitor the restaurants. After he departed one of our friends said that he envied Sal and I for the fruits of our labor, but would never work as hard as we had to get them. (The years of Sal being away has been compensated somewhat by the quality time we have in his retirement.)

I have not been bashful about striking up conversations with anybody at anytime, anywhere, and about anything. In an elevator in San Francisco we conversed with a total stranger who left us his telephone number and invited us to his home. In New Mexico, we stopped at a packed Mexican restaurant and located a booth. A nice-looking couple strolled in minutes later — locals, because nearly everybody greeted them — so I asked Sal to invite them over. They told us their life story. Sal still has their telephone number and address if we ever travel through there again. In New Mexico, again, on New Year's Eve, we drove to a hotel restaurant for dinner and saw an older couple by themselves. We struck up a conversation with them and carried it over into the bar where they shared about moving to New Mexico from Los Angeles, his illness, and their lonely lives. They asked us to stop at their home but we declined because the next day was a travel day. These are a couple of examples of why our lives are never dull.

I didn't know one iota about politics. We had always voted but were almost apolitical. After the Republicans first approached Sal to run, he told me about it that night at home and we laughed over the idea of a Representative Sal

Frederick. When three groups all asked him independently of each other he began taking it seriously. He wouldn't run unless I agreed to it, he said. To investigate the idea further Sal invited Sen. Glen Taylor and Glenda over for supper and later Rep. Mark Piepho. I picked their brains and asked Glenda the drawbacks from a spouse's viewpoint. Sal and I mulled their answers over before reaching a decision. I told him he would be good at it if he won.

We invited my mother and his folks over for dinner to break the news. They backed us. Later we telephoned all the children and they supported it as well. Molly, who was 18, was particularly forceful. While I was in the bathroom she walked in and sat down on the edge of the tub — she had a captive audience — and explained that if I said "no" Sal would resent me for it for the rest of our lives together.

Not much later Sal and I flew to Florida for vacation and looked up retiring Rep. Dick Wigley and his wife, Fran, who happened to be nearby at Pompano Beach. The day we stopped, Sal and Dick talked politics all afternoon, evening, and the next morning. Dick offered Sal his blessings. He had an axiom about politics that Sal and I took to heart: no matter what you do, you're going to upset fifty percent of the people fifty percent of the time.

In the Mankato area, voters expected their candidates to knock on doors and greet them individually. It was an exhausting job. While knocking in St. Peter on a hot humid night, my chest felt heavy and I began having trouble breathing. I wanted to stop but Sal talked me into another hour of it. I learned afterwards that I did have a heart problem. I worried about Sal's health too, as he trudged door-to-door in ninety-degree heat in late summer, sweating like a butcher, and then having to turn down a friend's invitation to "step on in for a drink" because he had so many other doors to knock on. It was grueling.

In St. Peter I didn't step up to the front door of one old house because its porch floor sagged and seemed unsafe. So I knocked on their side door. A voice hollered out for me to come in — and in I did, to the filthiest home I had ever seen in my life. In another incident in Kasota I was walking away from a door when it abruptly opened and a wet young man appeared dressed in a bath towel. I apologized for interrupting him and explained that I would have left the literature hanging on the doorknob but couldn't find one. He reached suddenly for the literature and his bath towel fell. A half block down the street later I was still laughing and Sal had to know why.

Of all the thousands of doors knocked on only two people had to show their dislike for Republicans. One of them had neighbors over when I knocked and she had to show off in front of her liberal companions, directing a mean-spirited diatribe at me. The second was a man who said he normally didn't speak to Republicans. People who directed nasty words at Sal hurt me more than him. He shrugged off their sharp words as simply "politics." A few comments originated from people I thought were friends, and I couldn't understand why they would want to rip Sal in public.

After we won we had to move to St. Paul. Dick Wigley said an apartment in Kellogg Square was best, and that many legislators, both DFL and Republican, had made it their session home. We followed his advice and rented a one-bedroom unfurnished apartment for the five-month stay. I wasn't used to city noise, such as police sirens, screaming drunks, belching buses — and being twenty-two stories in the sky.

Politics was all consuming; people outside of it couldn't understand that. It consumed every minute of every day. A politician had to be careful in what they said. Many were paranoid because of being misquoted so often and that made them more hesitate to speak freely. I found much of politics to be perception. The spin-doctors worked full time with misinformation and half-truths to confuse the voters as much as possible. Sal had "listening" hours where constituents could air their grievances in an environment blind to any party affiliation. Constituents were constituents, he felt, not party members, and if he could help them, he would.

Almost every night one lobbyist or another would invite us to a party and sometimes three such parties were scheduled the same night. At first it seemed wonderful: I didn't have to cook. But by late February the rush-rush of each day wore thin. As a freshman representative Sal felt he had to go to them all in order to learn more about the issues and for the lobbyists to learn about Sal. By his second term in St. Paul Sal was choosing the lobbyist parties by priority. We watched senior legislators and saw how they handled the parties. They walked in, pinned on their name badge, ate and then socialized. If Sal schmoozed before the meal he might have a great discussion but an empty belly by evening's end.

The most embarrassing thing Sal — and all the legislators — ever had to do was attend mandatory sexual harassment classes. Predictably, the classes made everyone into a paranoid mess, afraid to look at anyone of the opposite sex or compliment them on their dress or even their hairstyle. After one of the sexual harassment classes, an Iron Range Democrat who I knew well, was holding up the food line so I patted him on the butt and politely asked him to move. He latched onto my arm, held it high and yelled, "sexual harassment!" I nearly died from embarrassment.

In earlier times there weren't many personal divisions between members of both parties and it showed: on the floor, DFL and Republican members sat together, whereas today they sit on separate sides of an aisle. Sal was well liked by both parties because he wasn't a "rant and raver" as many legislators called them. The minute a rant and raver rose to speak it was time to take a nap because everybody knew what was coming. Sal would never do that even when asked.

After Sal left, the legislators, feeling pressure to do "something" to clean up government, outlawed lobbyist parties. What they did was a big mistake because those parties was the one place where DFL and Republican legislators could let their hair down and get to know each other as people. With the parties outlawed, the comradery between members of both parties went cold. Now legislators can't gel and mesh anymore. People talk about "partisanship" and that state government is too confrontational, well, it was made that way by well-meaning people trying to fix a problem with the wrong wrench. From those lobbyist parties I knew people as people, not as DFL or Republican.

Socializing at parties could only go so far in mending differences. One Democrat from the Iron Range had worked the mines like his father and grandfather. He was dead set against business because he thought the mine owners treated the miners horribly, which they did probably fifty years ago. He was a rant and raver against business. (Jim Rice, another DFL member, had two patented anti-business phrases: "a businessman would sneak into the mortuary and steal the pennies off his grandmother's eyelids just to satisfy his greed," and "when you turn 65, they'll take you out back and shoot you rather than give you a pension.") At one lobbyist party there was no place for Sal and I to sit except near the Iron Ranger and his wife, so she motioned for me to sit down with them. Sal shot me the look that only married people know. By then though, the Iron Ranger had downed a few drinks, felt a bit loose, and began talking about all the beautiful woodwork he did. He invited us over for the weekend to his home. As we were walking back to Kellogg Square that evening Sal said, jokingly, "It will be a cold day in Hell before we stay the whole weekend with him. Only one of us would come out alive."

When Sal lost in 1992 even some Democrats telephoned him to express their sympathies because many of them, on a personal level, didn't care much for his opponent. Sal was a people person, very outgoing and friendly while his opponent, to more than a few legislators, had a tendency to be aloof and reserved. He often exhibited what many felt was an attitude of "if I say it you better believe it because I said it." Imagine: Democrats offering their sympathies to us over losing the election.

The next morning we visited Sal's mother to inform her, but a nurse at her rest home had beaten us to it. His mother seemed happy, even joyful at the news. "You weren't yourself any more," she said, pointing at him with an index finger, "and you had lost your smile. You were working too hard. I'm glad you lost. I have my old Sal back." Later his brothers said the same. Looking back now the defeat was best from a personal standpoint. He had served eight long years and had been tiring of the stress and frustration.

One thing I have always questioned about the election process was why students are allowed to vote for local issues and legislation in the community where their school is located. A vast majority of them are only there for a short time and then move on. Hunters, snowbirds, travelers and handicapped persons must vote by absentee ballot in their home area, why are students given special privileges? According to former Secretary of State Joan Growe there is no way to check if these students vote at college and go home and vote again. In the 1990 election year, Mark Piepho heard of irregularities on the MSU campus. He sent registered letters to all who voted in that precinct and seventy-five came back with no such person residing there. There is voter fraud in Minnesota.

I miss my friends in the legislature, at Kellogg Square, the legislator's wives, the luncheons, shopping, and the movies. If our men were in session at night, many times the wives of legislators would eat dinner together. Out of our clique of eight, six were DFL, yet party affiliation didn't seem to matter to any of us. We were just friends. I'm a friend still with several Democratic wives.

Sometimes I knew more about what was going on at the Capitol than Sal. One noon I called and told him the session would end early that day because I had heard from several DFL wives that many of their husbands had tickets to the U of M hockey game. Sal disagreed and said they had too much on the agenda to dismiss early. He telephoned later and said I was right.

I enjoyed socializing. I was the first spouse of a minority party member to be elected president of the Rotunda Club, whose members were the male and female spouses of state legislators. The news even made the Star Tribune. It was through the Rotunda Club in the late '80s that I learned how Native Americans were becoming wealthy through casino gambling. A casino in Prior Lake asked if they could send a bus to the state capitol building to pick up Rotunda

Club members for an outing. They stuffed us with lunch at a restaurant by the river in Shakopee before guiding us to "Little Six Bingos" where they handed us free bingo cards. At another building we were given a five-dollar start at the slot machines. I won twenty-five dollars. An Indian woman showed us through their facility and told us that every man, woman and child in her tribe had received (if I remember correctly) $70,000 that year from gambling. All tribal members had to live on the reservation, which created a construction boom of beautiful three-bedroom homes and plush green lawns.

I asked our guide: "Why is it you're the only person of Indian heritage working here?" She said tribal members didn't have to work and that their children were dropping out of school because their future financial security had been guaranteed. She had tried persuading some of the kids to graduate, she said, but without an incentive it was like preaching to dead wood. They were living well but paying the price with the destruction of their families and their work ethic.

The Rotunda Club was also invited to a new women's prison in Shakopee. Their rooms were lovely, almost condo-like, and the nicer suites had kitchens where inmates could bake and cook. The longer the inmates were in the prison the more points they accumulated and the ones with more had bigger suites. All the inmates had access to a workout gym. I asked the tour guide if anyone had ever escaped — they had no fences — and she said yes, but all escapees had returned on their own. I said, "Why wouldn't they? They have it better here than on the outside." The tour guide sent a look that could kill. "Yes, Mrs. Frederick," she said, "but you can walk out of here and go home."

She wanted me, as president, to ask other Rotunda Club members to personally buy cake mixes as a gift for all the inmates. Later, when I said to Glenda Taylor, "it will be a cold day in Hell before we do that here," I didn't know the tour guide was behind me. She poked me in the back and told me I was being "narrow-minded." The women were having a hard time of it in prison, she said. I told her they should have thought of that before breaking the law.

105

Six months after the 1992 election a Rotunda Club member called to tell me that the club was falling apart and a year after that I learned it was defunct. Even though Sal had been out a year they wanted me to come back and organize it for them again as their president, which was a task I couldn't do because I didn't want to travel to St. Paul alone.

Terry Ventura, Loretta Langseth and Rose

I still attend Dome Club meetings, however, which are now for spouses of the House and Senate. In the spring of 1999, Terry Ventura invited the Dome Club to the governor's mansion for a tour. I was looking forward to seeing all my old friends. I liked Terry Ventura. She was attractive, funny, and down-to-earth, had common sense, and must really love Jesse to put up with all his nonsense. It seemed as if she was having the time of her life. She wore a cute white sweater and leather skirt that day. As the photographer was taking a picture of us, he suggested to Terry that she stick out her leg and lift her skirt a little. She did. Some of the older ladies in the back nearly had a heart attack.

The Venturas' dog was so fat he could barely walk, more of a waddler really. On the way out the governor's mansion I nearly stepped on him as he was stretching out in the sun. If I hadn't seen him I would have killed the governor's dog because I had high heels on.

I met Jesse only once, during his campaign for governor when he visited what was then the Mankato Civic Center. Afterwards we were invited to a party at the Intergovernmental Center across the street. Jesse had about twenty people in line waiting to talk with him. I went for a diet pop and while crossing the room ran into him. He said, "Rose, how are you?" I just said, "Hi." I went back to the table and asked everyone how Jesse knew my name. "It was on your name badge," Sal said. Duh!

I don't have regrets. I'm glad I didn't know at 17 what the future would bring with its twists and turns, because if I had known I probably wouldn't have married Sal. I would have been too afraid of waitressing, raising six girls, and being a legislator's spouse. I don't regret his foray into politics because we met and befriended people there who changed our lives for the better. The experience in St. Paul was an eye opener. I now realize the importance of becoming politically active, because if you don't do it somebody else will — and they will make the rules you must live by.

Sal's nine years of service on the National Restaurant Association board brought us in direct contact with people we would never have met in Mankato. George Burns dropped cigar ashes on me while entertaining us inside a private NRA suite. Former Dallas Cowboy Don Meredith spilled a mixed drink on my dress. A Pittsburgh Steeler, Franco Harris, gave me his autograph as a present for Molly's boyfriend. We were also privileged to meet President Ronald Reagan, then Vice President George and Barbara Bush, and the Bush's dog, Millie, at a luncheon at the Vice President's home. We've had our pictures taken with Tom Brokaw, Gen. Norman Schwartzkopf, Rush Limbaugh, Helen Reddy, Johnny Cash, Debbie Reynolds and others. Who would have thought all this would be in the future for a local Mankato girl from North Sixth Street?

This book would be remiss if we didn't tell you more about our six girls, fourteen grandchildren, and one great-grandson, born March 2000.

Kathryn Patricia, our first, was born in 1952 and lives in Minnetonka, Minn. We named her after my two sisters: Katie Keckeisen and Pat Nelson. Kathryn married Ernie Swartout and has three children, Chad, Jacob and Jessie, and one grandson, T.J. Swartout. Victoria Lynn, born 1954, married Kevin McLaughlin and has three children, Andy, Kyle and Molly Rose. They live in Mankato. Rebecca Anne, our third, born 1955, lives in Minnetonka, Minn., with her husband, Mitch Aspelund, and they have one son, Michael Marcel.

Mary Beth, born 1959, lives in White Bear Lake, Minn., with husband Denny Potz. They have four girls: Kimberlee Rose, Denise Marie, Anna Beth, and Kelly Rose. Margaret Rose (Peggy), our fifth born, named after my mother, Margaret Kelly, and myself, was also born in 1959. She lives in Kansas with husband Doug Milbrett. They have three children: Nicole, Bill and Sam. And finally, Molly Jo, the last born, was named after her great grandmother, Miriam Kelly (Molly is a derivative of Miriam). Born in 1963, she married Jesse Wolff in 2000 in our own backyard and now lives in Denver, Colorado, along with her step-son, Jack.

June 17, 2000: Molly Jo and Jesse Wolff

Apparently we were very busy from 1952 through 1963, and that along with two miscarriages in that time span. Sal didn't work all the time!

We celebrated our fiftieth wedding anniversary on a beautiful day, October 1, 1999. As Sal said then, "Our girls did us proud!" With Vicky as the mastermind and her husband, Kevin, designing the invitations, all the girls and their families worked to make it a most memorable event.

We started with a mass and renewal of our wedding vows at St. John the Baptist Catholic Church. Then we drove out to the Happy Chef North banquet room, which had been decorated beautifully by the girls with flowers, candles, and balloons. A scrumptious dinner preceded a program with our girls, sons-in-law and grandchildren all speaking. The evening finale was the performance of our six girls who sang a special song, to the tune of the Beverley Hillbillies theme, about our life. It was a showstopper that had us both laughing and crying. We feel very blessed having six healthy and happy girls and their growing families.

Sal started something fourteen years ago that his girls and I absolutely love. He offered to pay for us to go away every summer for about five days, which meant five wonderful days without husbands, kids, beds to make, dirty laundry and dishes, and ringing alarm clocks. The sisters get to bond and outlast their mother by staying up all hours of the night to talk, laugh, and reminisce. Mary Beth had suggested it way back when, and after weeks of planning and Sal's gracious offer to pick up that tab, it became a reality. In 2000, Molly, the new bride, came with us just three days after her wedding. (Jesse, her new husband, had said he could have her for the rest of his life. Nice guy.) We even met one of Sal's heroes, wrestler Vern Gagne, on one of the trips. Through it, the girls arranged for Vern to be a surprise guest at Sal's 65th birthday party. Boy, was he surprised.

The girls and their families treated us with a trip to Hawaii for our fiftieth wedding anniversary. Back in 1975, we did the same for Sal's parents with a trip to Rome for their fiftieth. In Rome, Pope paul VI ordained our friend, Father Joe Gannon, as a priest. An entire planeload of friends and relatives traveled along. Sal's dad was asked to serve mass for Father Gannon at one of the Vatican chapels at St. Peter's where he thought he'd died and gone to heaven. With our fiftieth we had come full circle.

Sal has said his life would be boring if I wasn't with him. That makes my heart happy to hear him say that. Sal and I will always be best friends, among other things.

* * * * *

The following poems and songs were presented to Sal and Rose for their 50th wedding anniversary.

WE ARE YOUR CHILDREN

*We are your children
You are a part of us
Whatever we have learned
We have learned from you
Whatever we have become
We have become, because of you
Wherever we go, you are with us
And wherever you are, we are also*

*We are your children
We have loved you
And learned from you
And now we live the lives
You have helped form*

*We are your children
And we thank you
For all the love you have given us
All the time you have shared with us
All the worrying you have done over us
You will always live in us
Because we are your children*

– All my love on your 50th, Kathi.

A POEM FOR SAL AND ROSE

Sal & Rose been married now
They claim it's 50 years.
They been in a lot of fist fights
And drank a lot of beers.

They have tried to change society
To make the world a better place
But in spite of all their efforts
It's still a sad disgrace.

But if they hadn't done what they did
Things would be a whole lot worse.
Instead of writing you this poem
I'd probably steal your purse.

– Rex MacBeth, writ by hand, October 2, 1999

50TH ANNIVERSARY SONG

(Sung by the "Sisters Six" to the tune of
"The Beverly Hillbillies" theme song.)

VERSE 1
Let me tell you all a story 'bout Rose and Sal
They met in '47 life was going pretty well
Sal's back from the Service, and was cooking up some food
Rose was baby-sitting the hotel chef's brood

Only Vicky: *Saulpaugh Hotel, fine food, ballroom dancing.*

VERSE 2
Well, after courting two years decided to get hitched
The honeymooners drove out west and saw some old snake pits
Then back they came to Katoland to start their married life
Sal cooking at the Topic, Rose was the young housewife

Only Vicky: *October 1, 1949, Ford Club Coupe, May Street and Thimble the dog*

VERSE 3
Three thousand dollar bills they borrowed, to start their own cafe
The Hidden Inn was just their first, and they were on their way
Soon the babies started coming, girl after girl
Two blondes, two redheads, two brunettes, but none of us had curls

Each will say their name: *Kathi, Vicky, Becky, Mary, Peggy and Molly Jo*

All together: *We are all the daughters of Marcel and Rose*

VERSE 4
Next came Frederick's Corner Café, Bretts Grill, and Newman Center
We moved on out to Southview Heights, and life was even better
The doors of Happy Chef opened in 1963
Rose chose that name because of Marcel's personality.

Only Vicky: *pancakes, breakfast anytime, located on Highway 169*

VERSE 5
Bob and Tom and Bill joined in, almost from the start
The Happy Chef was family-owned; Sal's brothers did their part
The restaurant now became a chain, and grew to 50 or more
Some have the talking statue, right outside the door

Only Vicky: *Push the button, hear the jokes, come on in for an ice cold Coke*

All together: *Dine at the sign of the Happy Chef*

VERSE 6
Then in 1967 moved out to the Ranch
Horses, hamsters, dogs and fish, and don't forget those cats
Trampoline and swimming pool, it is the place to be
Parties, weddings, holidays, with friends, and family

Only Vicky: *Indian Lake Ranch, country setting, beautiful view*

VERSE 7
Sal retired in '84 from the Happy Chef
Had faith in all his brothers, they'd continue its success
He jumped right into politics, became a State Rep
Rose was his first lady, St. Paul their new address

Only Vicky: *Kellogg Square, Capitol Building, pizza at the Savoy.*

VERSE 8
After serving four terms it came to be their last
Elections, sessions, lobbyists too, were now all in the past
For seven years they've done some traveling, south and to the west
Enjoying their retirement, this marriage is the best

Only Vicky: *Precious memories, laughter and tears, for fifty years*

VERSE 9
Now it's time to say thank you for kindly droppin' in
To celebrate this special day with Sal and Rose and kin
And to our mom and dad we say, we love you oh so much
Happy Anniversary, from the Frederick bunch

NAMES INDEX

Anderson, Kathy 74
Aspelund, Rebecca 108
Boeske, Lee 24,47
Boeske, Dorothy 24
Busse, Henry Jr. 52
Brokaw, Tom 107
Burns, George 107
Bush, Barbara 107
Bush, George 107
Carlson, Arne 81
Carstensen, "Sarge" 38
Cash, Johnny 107
Comstock, Walt 32
Cragun, "Dutch" 41
Crozier, Mildred Kelly 94
Dorn, John 76-77,79,81
Fasnacht, Evie 32,94
Frederick, Anne 35,95
Frederick, Bob 8,35-36,39,51,55-56,66,95-97
Frederick, Cletus 13,67
Frederick, Edward 8,24
Frederick, Gerald 8,10,24
Frederick, Mary Kramer 8
Frederick, Nicholas (Grandpa) 7-8,12-13
Frederick, Nicholas (Brother) 8,25
Frederick, Thomas 8,38-39,54,56
Frederick, Wanda Polaczyk 7-9,11,17
Frederick, William Henry 7-13,16-17
Frederick, William Henry, Jr. 8,39,93
Gagne, Vern 109
Gannon, Rev. Fr. Joe 109
Gutknecht, Rep. Gil 79
Harris, Franco 107
Henessey Air Force Tour 42
Holmes, Georgia 68
Jennings, Dave 79
Jorgenson, Earl 41
Kahn, Phyllis 77

Katoland Connection 82
Keckeisen, Jim 89
Keckeisen, Katie 107
Kelly, Margaret 29,108
Kelly, Miriam 108
Kitchenmaster, Bob 75
Krause, Ken 68
Kurth, Erv 36
Limbaugh, Rush 107
Lutz, Fred Jr. 65
Mankato Chamber of Commerce 76,82
Maslon, Jim 89
Matejcek, Patricia Frederick 8
McGowan, Jack 32
McGowan, Mac 32
McLaughlin, Victoria 108
McNamara, Freddy 8-9
McNamara, Ida 9,29
McNamara, Mike 9
Mickelson, Dr. John 89
Meredith, Don 107
Milbrett, Margaret Rose 108
Miller, Ray 27
Mn Restaurant Assn 41,47,50
Moe, Sen. Roger 80
MRCI Foundation 82
Muellerleile, Robert 37
Nat'l Restaurant Assn. 41-42,44,47,55
Negaard, Willie 69
Nelson, Pat 107
Ostrom, Rep. Don 81-82
Palmer, Floyd 73
Petersen, L.K. 31,33,36-37
Penny, Rep. Tim 83
Perpich, Rudy 81
Peters "Cal" 32
Piepho, Rep. Mark 65-66,81,100,104
Polaczyk, Francis 8

Potz, Mary Beth 108
Quist, Rep. Alan 81
Rachut, Helen Frederick 8
Radichel, Darlene 68
Reagan, Ronald 107
Reddy, Helen 107
Reynolds, Debbie, ... 107
Rice, Rep. Jim 103
Rotunda Club 105-106
Schneider, Jon 73
Scheurer, Clem 36
Schwartzkopf, Gen. Norman 107
Steensma, Rep. Andy 77
Storm, Rep. Julie 82-83
Swartout, Kathryn 107
Taylor, Sen. Glen 65,68,76,100
Taylor, Glenda 65,100,105
Thompson, Glen 66
Tonn, Martin 85-87
Ulman, Jim 52-53
Ventura, Gov. Jesse 106
Terry Ventura 106
Voelz, Dick 65
Watson, Jack 37
Wallrich, "Slim" 28
Wigley, Rep. Dick 65,100-101
Wigley, Fran 65,100
Wolff, Molly Jo 98,108